NEWTON PAGE

THE FINANCIER, LAW

His Scheme and Times

By

ANDRÉ COCHUT

NEWTON PAGE

NEWTON PAGE

The Financier, Law:
His Scheme and Times

By

André Cochut

Edited by Gavin Adams

First published as

*'The Financier, Law: His Scheme and Times.
A Graphic Description of the Origin, Maturity and Wreck
of the Mississippi Scheme.'*

First published by Newton Page 2010

1 3 5 7 9 10 8 6 4 2

© Newton Page 2010
All revised notes, text, headings, tables and index © Newton Page 2010
All Rights Reserved

Cover image from *Het Groote Tafereel der Dwaasheid*, Netherlands (1720)
'Result of the Wind Trade'

ISBN 978-1-934619-04-9
Library of Congress Control Number: 2010922209

Printed in the United States of America
Set in Adobe Garamond Pro

Except in the United States of America, this book is sold subject to the condition that it shall not, by way of trade or otherwise, be lent, resold, hired out, or otherwise circulated without the publisher's prior consent in any form of binding or cover than that in which it is published and without a similar condition including this condition being imposed on the subsequent purchaser.

The scanning, uploading and distribution of this book via the Internet or via any other means without the express permission of the publisher is illegal and punishable by law. Please purchase only authorized electronic editions, and do not participate in or encourage electronic piracy of copyrighted materials. Your support of both the author's and copyright holder's rights is appreciated.

INTRODUCTION

INTRODUCTION

The following recital presents incidents so extraordinary, and at the same time so little like truth to readers of our times, that it is necessary to furnish them with the means of verifying the facts stated.

The financial experiment of Law has been expounded, from different points of view, by Forbonnais, du Tot, Paris Duverney, and the anonymous author of a very remarkable manuscript, many copies of which exist in the public depositories, and especially in the National Library, under this title: "Supplément Français, No. 252."

Du Tot, the cashier of the Indian Company, is an admirer of the Scheme, which he has analysed incidentally in a book, entitled "Reflexions on Finance."[1] The manuscript above cited is also an apology for Law. Lemontey attributes it, we know not on what evidence, to the Count de Lamark, formerly Ambassador to Sweden, a man mixed up in all the great affairs of his time, and especially an attractive writer. Pâris Duverney, on the contrary, the rival and personal enemy of the Scotch financier, attacks him violently, while refuting du Tot's book, under the form of *An Examination*. The laborious historian

---

1. Reprinted, together with Law's works, in the "Collection of the Economists."

of our Finances, Forbonnais, preserves the impartiality of an English mind.

For the political and anecdotal part we have consulted Duhautchamp, an eye-witness, who wrote six volumes on the "History of the Scheme," and four volumes on the "History of the *Visa*," the Memoirs of Saint-Simon and those of Duclos, the lively summary of M. Thiers, a good study of Lemontey in his "History of the Regency," and many little squibs of the period, in print or in MS.

Finally, we have read, whilst writing the journals, or rather the *mementos*, written, under the impression of the events themselves, by excellent citizens who loved to record facts without troubling themselves about publicity. The National Library possesses three selections of this kind. First, "The Journal of Matthew Marais," published in extracts by the *Revue Rétrospective*. Marais, a Parliamentary advocate, aspiring to the French academy, has all the arch curiosity of a man of wit. The second journal is that of the advocate Barbier, in course of publication under the superintendence of *The Historical Society of France*. Barbier, though in a position to be well informed, is a sceptical and grumbling citizen. The third journal, specially devoted to the Regency, is without an author's name. It is attributed to Buvat, a writer attached to the Royal Library as a copyist. This same Buvat, who has acquired an historical celebrity from having discovered and revealed the conspiracy of Cellamare, is the commonplace echo of popular reports, which he reproduces without comment and without malice. Through him we became acquainted with the prejudices, and feel the emotions of the multitude. From bringing together these various authorities, the result, we think, is at least precise as to economical facts, and a correct picture of events.

André Cochut.

CONTENTS

BEFORE THE SCHEME	1
LAW	23
THE BANK	33
THE SCHEME	49
THE GOLDEN AGE	65
DISENCHANTMENT	95
THE FALL OF THE SCHEME	125
AFTER THE SCHEME	161
INDEX	183

CHAPTER I

BEFORE THE SCHEME

CHAPTER I

BEFORE THE SCHEME

Exhaustion of the Country—the Bernardines

The prosperous years of Louis XIV must have possessed a very dazzling splendour, since they were scarcely tarnished by the reverses and sufferings which afflicted the end of his reign. Few French princes, in civilized times, have handed down the country to their successors in such a state of utter ruin. Twice had desperate efforts been obliged to be resorted to in order to repel imposing coalitions, and obtain honourable treaties. After Colbert, the great King was not fortunate in the selection of his ministers of finance. Some were so incompetent as to confess it themselves, others of doubtful honesty. They existed only on loans and expedients; and as they did not pride themselves on good faith with contractors and capitalists, they could only obtain the assistance of these people by offering them profits proportioned to the risks of all kind they had to incur.

A single episode of financial history will show to what extremities they had reached. After the peace of Utrecht, the old King thought proper to make the royal star, so long obscured, once more dazzle the eyes of his people; he commanded that *fêtes* should take place at Fontainbleau. No *fêtes* without money, however. Four millions were demanded of the controller, Desmarets. But the treasury was empty, credit annihilated. The minister was in despair, and perhaps meditating some stroke like that which immortalised Vatel, when he perceived that his two men-servants secretly read his papers, and gave information to stockjobbers, with whom they had an understanding for speculation, of any news which might influence the course of public affairs. Without losing a moment, the minister caused to be privately made thirty millions worth of Treasury loan notes, a kind of Exchequer bill, which he entrusted to Samuel Bernard, the most influential of financiers. He then drew up the project of a lottery, tending to raise the current price of these securities; and taking care to have himself called away on pressing business, he took his departure, leaving his manuscript on his desk. Two hours afterwards the stockjobbers were informed of the magnificent projects of the minister for raising the value of the Treasury loan notes. These papers were immediately asked for, and so rushed after that they rose in a few days from 35 to 85 percent. Bernard took advantage of the opportunity to get rid of all the notes with which he had been entrusted, and the minister soon had in his hands a sum of money beyond what was required for the journey to Fontainbleau.

A few days after, the manoeuvre got wind, and the new notes, called by the public *Bernardines*, experienced a depreciation of two-thirds. It is true that the capitalists were not long in taking their revenge: the last loan negotiated by the great King was at 400 percent.

Louis XIV's Balance Sheet

During the last fourteen years of the reign of Louis XIV, the expenses had absorbed two billions, 870 millions of livres; the actual receipts had only produced 880 millions. Therefore, it had been necessary to borrow nearly two billions in the money of the time—a sum equivalent to three or four billions of our money.[1] A great part of this deficit had been consolidated in perpetual and life annuities, or paid in notes analogous to our Exchequer bills. From thence sprung a floating debt which, when the King died, in September, 1715, formed an arrear of 711 millions; the deficit already incurred for the current year was seventy-eight millions. The debt, therefore, immediately demandable, was raised to 789 millions of livres, at thirty livres the marc, which would represent 1,420 millions of our money. The Treasury was empty. Taxes were resisted in many of the provinces. The public service was declining for want of money. As for the public distress, it is sufficient to say that, during the winter then commencing, a considerable number of persons died in Paris of cold and hunger.

These facts having been made manifest in one of the first councils which followed the establishment of the Regency, some one proposed to declare frankly to the country that the position of the nation was desperate, and that it was utterly impossible for the young King to honour the engagements contracted during the previous reign. This advice was rejected with even more warmth by the Regent than by his counsellors. It was determined to aid the State by a series of measures tending to the same end, without having the odium of an avowed bankruptcy,

---

1. They made then only thirty livres, or francs, from an ingot of silver weighing one marc (245 grammes), whilst now we make fifty-four francs from the same weight.

[Therefore, as twenty-five francs of the present currency are about equal to £1 sterling, the English reader must reckon about fourteen livres of Louis XIV's time for the same sum; so that the national debt above mentioned was about 142 millions sterling.—Translator's Note.]

and admitting besides of the alleviations which were required by humanity and justice.

The *Visa* (or inspection)

The most urgent measure was to reduce the debt immediately payable, which consisted principally of a number of bills at short dates, signed in the name of the State (which was responsible) by the ministers, treasurers, receivers of contributions, chiefs of departments, and contractors. As these papers were negotiated at a constantly increasing loss, and had not cost their last holders a fourth part of their nominal value, it was thought that they might be reduced without injustice. A royal proclamation dated the 7th of December, enjoined all the holders to present their vouchers to a commission charged to revise them—that is to say, in plain language, to submit them arbitrarily to a greater or less reduction. After which, these papers, of so many different kinds, were to be replaced by a single sort of State Notes bearing 4 percent interest, and reimbursable at the times of their respectively falling due. 652 millions of debts were thus paid off with 250 millions of State Notes. But as the public had no guarantee against the abuse of this resource, the new securities fell the first day 40 percent; so that in the end, the possessor of a one hundred francs of paper on the death of Louis XIV, could not have got for it more than twenty francs in specie after the revision.

It was also attempted to derive a profit from the coinage itself, by reducing its intrinsic value about 43 percent. The annuities settled during the three preceding years were reduced one-half. Considerable retrenchments were made on all appointments, official salaries, and pensions. All these palliatives scarcely leaving their trace in the immensity of the wants, a more energetic remedy was attempted.

CHAPTER I

The Chamber of Justice

It was among the traditions of the old monarchy to choose the moment when *men of business* (this name was particularly applied to those who speculated in the collection of the revenue, the debts of the treasury, and public contracts) were in good feather to pounce down upon them, and make them disgorge. Without recalling the tragic histories whose last scenes took place at the Montfaucon gallows, exceptional tribunals were from time to time constituted, charged, it was said, with punishing usurers and squanderers of the public property. This admirable zeal scarcely ever burst forth, in truth, but when the treasury was empty. Sully, who had twice the weakness to consent to executions of this sort, frankly confessed his fault. "The little rogues," said he, "alone fall into the nets of justice: the great and powerful thieves find means to escape." After having begun by ill-using capitalists and contractors, Colbert tried to repair his fault by showing them great respect. It is said that it was, thanks to his recommendation, that the financiers were spared by Molière.

Men who had speculated on the wants of the exchequer and the supplies of the army, from the commencement of the century, were the only ones who had made a profitable business, and their luxury seemed like an insult to the general distress. The nobility were especially galled by it. Besides, their wealth was exaggerated when it was supposed that, without ruining them, they might be curtailed of 800 millions. The Duke de Noailles, who had a fixed opinion on the subject, caused it to prevail in the financial council. The affair was managed like a little *coup d'etat*. On the 9th of February, 1716, a certain number of financiers were taken away from their homes and conducted to the Bastille. At the same time postmasters were forbidden to supply chaises or horses to anyone. It was forbidden, *under pain of death*, for farmers of the revenues, under-farmers, collectors, sub-collectors, as well as to all their partners (that is to say, sleeping-partners) and clerks, to go more than a league from their residence. After these precautions appeared the edict which established a Chamber of Justice for the punishment of misappropriations committed by those who had been directly or indirectly in connection with the affairs of the state since the year 1689—that is to say, during a period of twenty-seven years.

The tribunal was composed of six Master Accountants and of four Counsellors of the Excise Court under the direction of Messieurs Lamoignon and Portail, President-Judges in Parliament, and with Mr. de Fourqueux as Attorney-General. The installation took place on the 14th of March, in the hall of the Convent of the Grands-Augustins, on the spot where has since been erected the Market of la Vallée. The gentlemen of the long robe were at this period filled with the passions and prejudices of the multitude against those who made a trade of money, and who acquired wealth by operations out of the ordinary routine of commerce. Speculations in public securities and in the fluctuations of the stocks, so much in favour and so lucrative nowadays, inspired them with an instinctive horror. After having pointed out the different categories of suspected persons, in an address pronounced at the opening of the chamber, and a copy of which has been preserved, d'Aguesseau adds:—"There is another class of men among whom there must be found some guilty ones. These are the usurers, to whom the trade in stocks has given birth in darkness and obscurity. They have raised sudden fortunes, the foundations of which they have robbed from the public. You will dive into these foundations, gentlemen, and you will destroy these detestable edifices of iniquity."

CHAPTER I

The Informers

With these intentions, nothing was neglected to give an overwhelming power to the redoubtable tribunal. All public and private accountants were ordered to communicate such registers, accounts, books, and papers as were of a nature to enlighten this inquisition of fortunes. Persons who had realised any profits during twenty-seven years were obliged to produce the most minute balance sheet of their property and acquisitions. Notaries and payers of annuities were summoned to give, officially, explanations of the affairs in which they had been agents.

Every false declaration entailed the punishment of the galleys for life on men, and nine years banishment on women, besides the confiscation of their property. Rewards were offered for information—that of a servant against his master or a son against his father—and it was forbidden on pain of death to speak ill of the informers. Let us say that, to the honour of our own time, such things are so far removed from ourselves that they appear incredible. We must, therefore, furnish proofs which result from the royal declaration of the 17th March:—

"It shall be lawful for all persons who may wish to give information, even to the lackeys and other servants of those who are amenable to our said Chamber, to give such information in their own names, or, if it pleases them, under feigned names, giving at the same time clear and certain proofs of the facts which they denounce. We forbid all our subjects, *under pain of death*, to ill-treat, or speak ill of the informers."

The bait offered to traitors was very seductive. They allowed them the "fifth part of the fines and confiscations adjudged to the State, and the tenth part of the property hidden, secreted or fraudulently carried away." A servant could make himself a rich man in a quarter of an hour without even losing his place. Clerks were posted in different quarters of the town to receive voluntary declarations and secret notices, and measures were taken so that informers, desirous of maintaining their incognito, might handle the price of their infamy without blushing. Abominable betrayals were undoubtedly committed.

Invested with arbitrary power, the Chamber of Justice proceeded in an expeditious manner without publicity, without defence, and without appeal. The suspected man was cited before the Court, or even taken from his house, and imprisoned as a precaution, if the case imputed to him bore the character of an offence. One of the judges inquired into the affair through authentic papers or anonymous information, and on his report the court pronounced its punishments, which might extend from a fine even to death. From time to time, as if to make an example, it ordered the sale, for the benefit of the State, of property of the condemned and afforded a show to the multitude, by causing to be put up to auction, in some public place, the horses, carriages, wines, pictures, furniture, and costly dresses which had excited so much envy.

Corporal Punishments

It is not easy to satisfy the enmity of the lower orders: they must have victims to torture. Fate appeased them with two collectors of the taxes formerly levied on the communities of arts and handicrafts, named Gruet and Le Normand. They were accused of having falsified public documents in order to burden the taxpayers; and they alleged in defence, that they had done so by order of their superiors. However this may have been, their punishment, which did not let them off with confiscation and the galleys, offered scenes calculated to demoralise the people. The impression was so vivid that large engravings were struck of the occasion. There are seen the condemned led through the streets on foot, in their shirts, ropes round their necks, tapers stuck in their handcuffed hands, tied behind a wretched cart, which is drawing them towards the places where they must make the *amende honorable*, and from thence to the pillory. On their back is hung a placard, on which is written in large letters, *Robbers of the People*—and the people at the doors, at the windows, on the posts, on the roofs, enjoy their vengeance in yelling, insulting, and singing, as the condemned pass by:—

> *C'est lui qui pour une pistole*
> *Vous faisait cent Ecus de frais:*
> *Ou diable allait il a l'ecole*
> *Pour savoir d'aussi beaux secrets?*[2]

The pillory was a kind of little turret, surmounted by a horizontal wheel turning on a pivot. Holes bored in the band of the wheel gave passage to the head and hands of the sufferer, and from time to time the apparatus was turned round, so that the face, abandoned to the outrages of the mob, should be successively seen on every side. Three times Gruet was put in the pillory, and three times the market women came yelling to throw mud in his face, whilst the unfortunate wretch cried out that his only crime was having been too faithful to the orders of the minister Desmarets, and of the lieutenant of police, d'Argenson. On the third day the cold was so keen, that the sufferer had been allowed to throw a little clothing over himself. Enraged at this indulgence, these viragoes stopped up the kennels, so that the condemned should be obliged to walk barefoot on the frozen mud.

---

2. Tis he who, for one pistole,
 Made you a hundred crowns expenses:
 Where the devil went he to school
 To learn such capital secrets?

Le Normand had to endure still more. After the tortures of the pillory, he was conducted to la Tournelle, naked, on foot, and in very cold weather, waiting till he should be sent to the galleys. "At la Tournelle the guard tied him up to a tree in the middle of the court, so as to place him in sight of all those who flocked in crowds, and each of whom willingly gave four sous to the jailor so as to have the pleasure of reproaching the condemned man with his embezzlements, and with the vexations he had caused them. To which he made no reply, though some of them brutally struck him on the head."[3] Similar executions took place in the provinces. It is only a hundred and thirty-six years since such scenes, authorised by power, and approved by the most estimable men, took place in France!

There were also some condemnations to death, amongst others that of Paparel, treasurer of the King's household. He was accused, among other rogueries, of having appropriated to his own profit a tenth of the payments made to the bodyguard: above all, they regarded it as a felony that he had, during the late wars, invested 1,600,000 livres in foreign funds. But Paparel was son-in-law to the Marquis of Lafare, the captain of the Regent's guards, and one of his favourites. He obtained successive alleviations of his penalty, and at last got off with the loss of half his property.

The Great Financiers

It was not the heads of rich people, but their purses, that were aimed at. The affair[4] which made the most noise was that of Bourvalais. For a long time the nobility had endured the

---

3. Journal of Buvat.

4. Paul Poisson, called Bourvalais from the name of an estate which he had purchased, was the son of a poor Breton peasant He had been a footman like most of the financiers of his day.

splendour of his luxury as an insult. Public report made it a crime in him to have invested in foreign banks 1,200,000 louis d'or—a sum equal to thirty-four millions of francs of our time. Six large wagons, three of them loaded with plate, which was coined into money for the benefit of the State, could not carry away all the furniture of his fine hotel in the Place Vendôme. But is it surprising that a man who had been the principal army contractor during twenty years of war, should have amassed treasures? Guilty or not, Bourvalais was carried off from his family and his business, and closely guarded in one of the dungeons of the Bastille. It was a sad spectacle—that of a man so basely flattered the day before, and now denounced by his own lackeys and by his friends in the hopes of snatching a rag from his spoils. A servant went and declared to the magistrates that he had dug a secret place in the house: another, that he had sewn up 150,000 livres in notes in his master's clothes. A friend who had been entrusted with the care of a casket containing jewels of the value of 200,000 crowns, carried it to the Chamber of Justice.

"A priest of St. Sulpice, named Rey, to whom Bourvalais had confided some important affairs went and denounced him, and declared that he had 500,000 livres of bonds on the city of Paris, in his name. The sum was confiscated to the benefit of the King, with the exception of 100,000 livres, which were granted to the priest as his right for the information."[5]

Nevertheless, as no materials were found for criminal proceedings against Bourvalais, he was released after a year of close confinement, leaving for himself and his wife a capital of 450,000 livres clear of all debts. All the rest of his property, valued at more than four millions (that is to say, about eight millions of our money) was declared forfeited to the King. In this category was included the fine hotel on the Place Vendôme,

---

5. Historical Recreations of Dreux de Radier.

of which Bourvalais had made a splendid residence, and where it was found convenient to install the Chancellerie de l'Etat, which has remained there from that time. It will be admitted that it is not in this manner our law now proceeds in cases of expropriation for the sake of public utility.[6]

The buildings where the printed books of the National Library now are were acquired at almost the same price. There was in 1704 a man named Chatelain employed as groom in the convent of Metz. Like all lads who felt themselves possessed of ambition and intelligence, Chatelain entered the service of an army contractor, and was soon in a position to undertake business on his own account. A short time before the death of Louis XIV, he had at his command sixty mounted clerks scouring the country to collect corn destined for the army. With the view of establishing warehouses in Paris he had bought in the Rue de Richelieu, close to his own dwelling, a portion of the great Hotel Mazarin, to which was then given the name of the Hotel de Nevers. The bargain had just been concluded at the price of 370,000 livres in hard cash, when the new proprietor was arrested on secret information which attributed to him a fortune of eleven millions. He got off, after several months imprisonment, with a fine of 2,500,000 livres, (or four millions and a half of present money,) in which was included the value of his immoveable property. Buvat who, in his capacity of *employé* at the library, took an especial interest in this affair, writes, under the date 11th of November, 1716:—"The Regent approves of the proposal made to him by the Abbé de Louvois to remove the King's Library to the Hotel de Nevers."

The rule which the Chamber of Justice appears to have followed, when there was no plainly characterised offence, was to deprive the speculators of four-fifths of their property,

---

6. Bourvalais was reinstated by a decree of the 5th September, 1718, which restored to him a portion of his property.

deducting what they possessed on commencing business. It showed itself inflexible with upstarts who had not yet attained a firm footing; but it admitted arrangements with the princes of finance who were already allied to great families: with Samuel Bernard, the great financial power of Europe, who had enjoyed the honour of being courted by Louis XIV: with the collector of revenue, Prondre, father-in-law of a La Rochefoucauld: with Crozat, who, from a little clerk—it is even said a footman to the receiver, Penantier—had become the first merchant in France, and had just betrothed his daughter to the Count d'Evreux, of the princely house of Bouillon. These influential men were permitted to tax themselves, and they were seen, in some sort, informing against one another, each appearing to fear that he should mulct himself more than his brethren. Samuel Bernard offered nine millions in hard cash,[7] that is to say, 16,200,000 francs of our times; but he insisted that Crozat, who had the audacity to call himself as rich as he, should pay a similar sum. Crozat got off for 6,600,000 livres, (or 11,880,000 francs,) declaring that it was scandalous that Prondre should be let off with only 1,900,000 livres, (or 3,400,000 francs). Lastly, Bernard, Crozat, and Prondre, reunited to demand, that a certain Menou, taxed only at 2,700,000 livres in hard cash, should give at least double that sum.

Spoliations

The Chamber of Justice having been instituted to curtail fortunes acquired by criminal means, the very inscription of one's name on its records might seem to have been a mark of infamy. However, we are astonished to find among the number persons entrusted with the highest offices, and who still

---

7. He seems only to have paid six, doubtless to put himself on the same level with Crozat.

retained them. Durey de Vieux-Cours, president of the Grand Council, who had admitted possessing a capital of 3,600,000 livres, was taxed at 3,200,000; they deigned to leave him a sum of 400,000 livres. A M. de Rancy, keeper of the royal treasure, was marked for 4,200,000 livres. The president of the Chamber of Accounts, many presidents of Courts of Request, a secretary of the King, the treasurer-general of the navy, judges and lawyers, a number of farmers-general of the revenue, and public collectors, nearly all the merchants interested in the supplies of the army, were taxed at considerable sums. They even went to the extremity of commencing proceedings against the ex-chancellor, Pontchartrain, accused of possessing between himself and his son two millions and a half per annum. If these men were rogues, why leave to them the administration of justice, and the management of the revenues of the kingdom? If their property was legally acquired, why take it from them?

It was because this inquisition on misappropriation had changed its character. Such is the danger of all inquiries of this kind. There is so much interest in finding out the guilty, that in the end the latter are seen on all sides. The operations of the Chamber of Justice tended to make a kind of forced loan, not only from men scandalously enriched, but from all who were suspected of being in good circumstances.

An edict of the 18th of September, 1716, whilst mitigating corporal and degrading punishments, gave a much wider scope to the pecuniary inquisition. A delay of ten days' grace only was allowed to men of business, as well as to their partners and associates, "to make a declaration of their property; after which, the fine imposed by the judges having been paid, they would be summoned to recognise and confess that they retained the remainder as a simple favour of the King's goodness, and without having deserved it."

A war-treasurer, Dumoulin, was condemned to the galleys for

having concealed a portion of his fortune. Fresh encouragements were given to the espionage of servants:—"A footman having informed that his master had hidden one million in specie in a place in his house, the Regent ordered a tenth part of it to be given to the man."[8] From such examples there was a fresh outburst of information. The widow of a councillor was betrayed by her son. A landlord, denounced as a secret hoarder of money, received a visit from a commissary of the Châtelet, accompanied by a party of masons armed with pickaxes and hammers; and after a thorough search of the furniture, they set to work, probing the walls, digging in the cellars, unpaving the courtyards, and turning up the garden.

Commercial Morals

Rich people, or to speak more correctly, the enriched citizens, offered only a passive resistance to these insults. Each one invented some trick to save his own property; but the pitiless tribunal nearly always seized a second time on those under its jurisdiction. To prevent precious goods from being turned into cash, goldsmiths were forbidden to purchase plate, and engravers to obliterate names or arms. Many annuitants transferred their vouchers to persons of trust—such as priests, pious virgins, old and faithful servants. These trusts were put a stop to by a threat of suppressing all annuities of doubtful origin. Bankers had recourse to all sorts of stratagems to pass their cash over to foreign countries. On one occasion fourteen carts were stopped on the frontier laden with casks of wine, in the centre of which were suspended little barrels filled with louis d'ors to the amount of five million livres. So much loss to the owners. One other fact, handed down in contemporary memoirs, will complete the picture of the commercial morals

---

8. Facts noted down, day-by-day, in the Journal of Buvat.

of this period.

A rich merchant of the St. Martin district, named Vermalet, feared, rightly or wrongly, the search of the Chamber of Justice:—"This is the way," says Duhautchamp,[9] "he set to work to make his escape to Holland with his gold and silver. He dressed himself as a peasant, and having bought a little cart, drawn by a horse, he loaded it with hay and straw. In this turn-out he boldly set forth on his journey, selling his hay and straw at the prices offered him, and bargaining no more than was necessary to hide his real game. Having sold all, he reloaded with fresh goods, and recommenced his manoeuvre. Avoiding the highways as much as possible, he endeavoured to arrive, so as to pass the night in villages rather than towns; and as he could not lose sight of his cart, where all his treasure was, he made it his lodging place. His terrified imagination made him always fancy that the archers were pursuing him. Judge of his perplexity, when one day he saw seven or eight of them really appear, and one of them leaving the rest came up to him at full gallop, commanding him to stop. He believed himself lost past all help. Luckily for him, they only wanted to take his cart for one man of the troop, who had been dangerously wounded by a fall. Everything considered, Vermalet thought it best to do the thing with good grace. He was obliged to retrace his way as far as a village where he had passed the preceding night. He was fortunate enough to be asked no questions; he would probably have been recognised and imprisoned, as the archers were directed to arrest all who were suspected of a wish to leave the kingdom. In short, he got off with a fright only, and arrived safely on the frontier with all his property, and without any other accident. After that time he managed his affairs so well, that he returned to France, where he lived in a most expensive

---

9. History of the Scheme, vol. i p. 189.

style."

Tracked, ruined, and to crown the evil, vilified by the multitude, who applauded the violence of power, many financial men gave themselves up to frightful resolves. There were a great many suicides. One unfortunate man set fire to his papers and his furniture, and stabbing himself with a dagger, threw himself into the flames. The collector of the free-fiefs of Orleans, summoned before the Chamber of Justice, lost his senses, and threw himself into a well. Justice had the corpse drawn out of the well, gravely went on with the proceedings, and condemned it to be hanged by the feet, and afterwards drawn on a hurdle. But this barbarous sentence was quashed by Parliament, which authorised the family of the deceased to bury him honourably.

The inquisition extending itself by degrees from collectors and extortioners by profession, to all those who, far and near, had dabbled in financial matters and contracts, the alarm became general. The rich feared to render themselves suspected by their expenditure; all business transactions were stopped. After one year's trial, the Chamber of Justice had become as odious to the public as it had been at first popular. It was alleged, besides, that many of those judges who were so fierce at starting had become quite tame, and that it would not be inappropriate to establish a zealous Chamber to judge the Chamber of Justice. Saint-Simon says briefly of the president Lamoignon:—"He gained a great deal of money in it, and disgraced himself." This magistrate is probably the one whom the public saluted with the name of "keeper of the pails,"[10] because he had the shamelessness to put on his table some silver pails, formed to

---

10. Seaux-pails—is pronounced precisely like sceaux, seals. Hence "garde des seaux," the title mockingly bestowed on Lamoignon, sounded like "garde des sceaux," keeper of the seals—a high office under the French monarchy.— Translator.

cool wines, which were part of the confiscation he had himself pronounced against Bourvalais.

At length the necessity was recognised of suspending the proceedings against the financiers, and on the 20th of March, 1717, the Chancellor came and closed the Chamber of Justice with an address, in which he confessed the discredit of its jurisdiction.

"The people have fallen," he said, "into a kind of consternation, which makes the political body languish, and such is their inconsistence, that they have passed suddenly from the hatred they felt for the accused to compassion for the misery to which they find them reduced: they accustom themselves to believe them innocent when they see them too long unfortunate."

Produce of the Fines-Protectors

The proceedings altogether had been much less productive than had been expected. About six thousand persons possessing, according to their own declarations, 1,200 millions of property (in hard cash equal to 2,160,000,000 francs of our time,) had been heard, but all had not been condemned. The number of the condemned did not exceed four thousand four hundred and ten. They had confessed to 713 millions of property, which, deducting debts and sums not subject to the fine, did not represent according to them more than 400 millions clear. The fines were distributed into nineteen lists of names which appeared successively. Beside a colossal fine, one may be found which descends below 1,000 livres.

Altogether, on the 400 millions net, belonging to the 4,410 persons adjudicated on, the fines and confiscations pronounced exceeded 219 millions. But it is a mistake to suppose that the State profited to the extent of this sum. In the month of June, 1717, only seventy millions had been recovered, and it was with great difficulty that half the fines were got into the Exchequer.

It was ascertained that some great persons had received large sums from the condemned, whose penalties they had procured to be moderated, and at length solicitations in favour of financiers became a special kind of industry. At court everyone traded on his influence, and thanks to this concurrence, protections were offered to procure an abatement of fines. It is related that an individual fined 1,200,000 livres, received a visit from a nobleman who promised to have it cancelled for a perquisite of 300,000 livres. "Upon my honour, Count," said the collector, "you have come too late: I have just made a bargain with the Countess for 150,000 livres."

Political Agitation

Certainly the rogues were in the majority among those brought under the jurisdiction of the Chamber of Justice, and nevertheless, as with all measures which bear the character of spoliation and violence against capitalists, the financial inquisition produced only the effect of rendering money scarce, suspending trade, and doubling the embarrassments of the Exchequer. Assistance was no longer to be obtained from private individuals, even on the conditions formerly insisted on by the usurers, whom they had just been disgracing. The sole and only resource which seemed to remain was to depreciate the coinage.

An edict of the month of May, 1718, therefore commanded a fresh recoining of specie in the proportion of sixty-five livres to the marc of silver. This was another depreciation of 50 percent on money, already reduced in December, 1715. The crownpiece of three livres ten sous, which weighed an ounce at the death of Louis XIV, was henceforth to weigh less than half an ounce. Evidently this operation was ruinous to trade. The Parliament of Paris which was, besides, only waiting for a legitimate pretext for opposition to the Regent, assembled in the Palace of Justice, the Supreme Courts, the most notable men of commerce, and of the Bank, on the 15th of June, 1718; it issued a decree forbidding everyone to tender or receive money of the new coinage, and, by the next morning, the annuitants of the Hotel de Ville refused to accept the depreciated louis d'or.

The Regent quashed this decree as outraging the royal authority, and forbid printers, under pain of death, to multiply it by printing it. Parliament had copies made of it on stamped paper, and delivered them to brave citizens who went and placarded them in the cross-ways, in spite of the soldiers who traversed the streets with orders to fire on the bill-stickers. From Paris, as the focus, the fire spread to the provinces. The Parliaments of Rouen, Aix, Bordeaux, and Rennes forbade people to work at the new coinage, or even to receive it. There was a rising in several places. Blood flowed at Besançon. Squibs, satirical or impassioned, (which they called *tocsins*,) began to circulate, as in the days of the Fronde. The plots of Cellamare were hatched in the dark. The faithless freebooters, whom legitimate princes then enrolled, only waited for a signal. France was threatened with seeing once more, during the minority of Louis XV, the scenes which had thrown a shadow over the infancy of Louis XIV.

A pacific experiment diverted all these commotions. A stranger, established for the last three years in France, and skilful in insinuating himself into the best society, had constantly declared that the financial crisis would occasion great disorder, that the expedients proposed—bankruptcy, the *Visa*, recoining the money, the Chamber of Justice—would only increase the evil, and that the only remedy consisted in certain practices which he called vaguely, *credit*. This man had made, at his own expense, and with a rare disinterestedness, an experiment of his notions. Success spoke in his favour: the hour for this celebrity had now arrived.

CHAPTER II

LAW

CHAPTER II

LAW

- His Birth and Education—Morals and Doctrines

"A Scotchman, of I don't know what birth, a great gambler and great *combiner*, and who had won largely in the different countries where he had lived, had arrived in France during the last days of the late King. He was named Law; but when he was better known people were so accustomed to call him *Lass*, that his name of Law disappeared. People spoke of him to the Duke of Orleans as a man profoundly conversant with matters of banking, commerce, the fluctuations of money, currency, and finance. This made him desire to see him." Does not this first sketch of Law's portrait, drawn by Saint-Simon, make you desire, like the Regent, to know him?

John Law was born in Edinburgh, in April, 1671. Was he, or was he not, of noble descent? This was a very grave question for his contemporaries, who fought over it for a long while; for us it scarcely possesses the interest of curiosity. The mother of the celebrated financier, Jane Campbell, was distantly connected, it was said, with the ducal house of Argyll, one of the most illustrious in Scotland. His father, William Law, had kept a goldsmith's shop in Edinburgh; but this trade did not then consist, as in our days, only in making precious metals into articles of luxury or use. The goldsmiths were, at the same time, changers and bankers. The frequent alterations which the coinage underwent made their intervention necessary in most transactions. The national or foreign coins, which were entrusted to them to estimate their value, were commonly left in their hands: often they were even requested to put them out to interest. Becoming thus the principal agents in payments and loans, the goldsmiths had a considerable influence in business. These details will suffice to show in what rank of the social hierarchy Law was born. Without being exactly noble, he was born in those high commercial circles where the speculator verges on the man of quality. Besides, by purchasing the two estates of Lauriston and Randleston, his father had handed down to each of his children the right of adding a landed title to his name.

John Law was fourteen years old when the worthy goldsmith died. The widow, who appears to have been a very superior woman, fostered, by the direction she gave to her son's studies, the tastes which the latter evinced for the exact and speculative sciences. On attaining his majority, Law found himself master of an inheritance which secured his independence. With intellectual culture, power of oratory, an imposing appearance, a charm of countenance, a rare skill in all bodily exercises, he united in himself all those qualities of which the type of a perfect gentleman was then formed.

Towards the year 1694, a taste for adventure led the young Scotchman to London. He there spent his elegant leisure in gambling, love intrigues, and frequenting political circles. At this time, the formation of the Bank of England, the theme of a very active controversy, offered Law an excellent subject for study. Unfortunately, having fought a duel with a gentleman named Wilson and mortally wounded him, he was tried and condemned to death. The more severe the penalty for misdeeds of this kind, the more easily was clemency shown—Law obtained his pardon. The family of the deceased having made a great noise about such an indulgence, the culprit was obliged to be seized again, doubtless for example's sake, for it is probable that they left him opportunities of escaping from prison. Prudence forbidding him to remain in London after his escape, he left England with the intention of travelling on the continent. He was then twenty-four years of age.

In the course of a few years Law visited Amsterdam, Paris, Venice, Genoa, Florence, Naples, and Rome. Although this life of experiment and adventure soon diminished his patrimony, he found means of carrying on life, assuming always the easy graces of a libertine cavalier, the magnanimous coolness of a regular gamester, and the penetration of political roué, making himself above all remarkable for his innate quickness at solving financial problems. Through calculating the eventual chances, gambling became a very lucrative profession to him. Wherever he exercised this sort of industry his constant good fortune made him suspected. But there is nothing to justify us in believing that he ever deserved those wounding aspersions which were scarcely spared him. Saint-Simon, who watched him closely on this point, bears witness to his honesty. His power of calculation, and his imperturbable coolness, gave him a natural superiority over the madmen whom the passion of play blinded. The habit of speculating on other people's want of skill, far from drawing unfavourable notice on a man, was authorised by the manners of the times. Louis XIV, the oracle of propriety, liked people about him to play high: it showed their good birth. No one was shocked at seeing the Portuguese Ambassador gain 1,800,000 livres in a single night from the

Duchess de Berry, the daughter of the Regent.

The chances of the green table being insufficient to satisfy a lofty intellect, Law directed his attention to the essence and functions of specie, and the mysterious power of credit. At Amsterdam he associated with merchants to make himself acquainted with the resources of commerce. Gambling in the public securities, a dark trade whose secrets were then known to a very few adepts, procured him in a short time considerable profit. By instinct he set to work to sketch out the laws of the phenomena which he observed. Without exactly becoming what we now call an economist, he acquired ideas on economical subjects that most statesmen were then deficient in. At a time of crisis and almost general distress, he believed himself called to the office of reformer, not doubting that European politics would, sooner or later, afford him an opportunity of putting his theories to the test.

It was natural that he should first offer his services to his own country. Scotland, then independent, was beginning to suffer from an industrial fever, which some years later troubled England. Many projects of banks, colonisation, discoveries, and commercial societies resulted often in rash and ruinous enterprises; but from time to time they called forth the elaboration of economical ideas. From 1700 to 1707, Law took an active part in this movement; and it was during this period that he composed his principal work "Considerations on Currency and Commerce,"[1] a work which he had presented to the Scotch Parliament by the Duke of Argyll, and which was warmly supported by a political coterie called *The Squadron*. A large majority rejected the project, deciding against innovations in matters of finance. Law had proposed the formation of a

---

1. This Pamphlet, written first in English, was translated into French about the year 1790.

territorial Bank, which should give to the Scotch landlords paper having a forced currency to the extent of a certain portion of the value of their estates. Suppress the forced currency; facilitate the negotiation of these territorial notes, and you will have the *credit-foncier* so much in favour in our time.

Discouraged by his bad reception from his own countrymen, Law recommenced his vagabond life. After a year's stay in Brussels "he came to Paris, where he made a good appearance, which he maintained by play. He generally played faro at the house of la Duclos, a tragic actress in fashion, though he was constantly invited by princes and nobles of the highest rank, as well as by the most celebrated academies, where his noble manners distinguished him from other gamblers. When he went to Poisson's, in the Rue Dauphine, he took there no less than two bags full of gold, which made a sum of about 100,000 livres. It was the same at the Hotel de Gesvres in the rue des Poulies. His hand not being able to grasp the quantity of gold he wished to stake at once, he had counters struck of the value of eighteen louis each. In spite of his good manners, he however made enemies, who caused him to be suspected by the government, and especially by M. d'Argenson, lieutenant-general of police. This magistrate ordered him to quit Paris, under the pretext that he knew how to play too well at the games he had introduced into this capital."[2]

Gain only occupied the second place in the calculations of the foreigner. His dissipated life, which brought him into contact with the highest society, furnished him with opportunities of developing his brilliant theories, and of gaining converts to them among men of high standing. It was thus that he even reached the Duke of Orleans. This young prince, gifted with a powerful imagination, and fond of novelty, experienced, more than any one else, the kind of fascination that Law produced:

---

2. History of the Scheme by Duhautchamp, Vol. i.

he spoke of him to the Controller-General, Desmarets, as a man of fertile resources, and worth consulting. The connection which sprung up between the minister and the foreigner was suddenly broken by the order which the latter received to quit Paris in four-and-twenty hours.

Leaving France, Law went to Genoa, Rome, Venice, Florence, Turin, and many German courts, watching everywhere for an opportunity to offer his *Scheme* to governments whose finances were embarrassed, experiencing refusals more or less polite, consoling himself for his political failures by play and stockjobbing, winning enormous sums, and always ending by being suspected by the police, and getting himself ignominiously expelled.

This singular course of life had brought the Scotch adventurer to his forty-fourth year, when he was informed at the same moment of the death of Louis XIV, and of the elevation to the Regency of the Duke of Orleans, the very man who appeared to have best understood his ideas. It was the finest turn of the game that fortune had ever presented him. A fortnight had not passed before he was in Paris with all he possessed. The kind of life he was about giving up had been so profitable to him, that after extravagances which equalled those of the highest nobles, he was able to realise 1,600,000 livres in hard cash, that is to say, 2,680,000 francs of our money.

We have now told all that is known of the antecedents of an extraordinary man, who was about to inoculate France with a mania unexampled in history. In what, then, did this discovery consist, which his contemporaries have called *The Scheme*, as if they saw in it a complete whole, the last word of social science?

Read the analysis of the eight or ten writers who have endeavoured to expound dogmatically Law's principles, and you will be astonished to find them often in contradiction not only with each other, but with Law himself. It is (and this looks like a paradox) because this innovator, who has become so famous for his *Scheme*, never had, properly speaking, any *Scheme* at all. He has nowhere laid down a theory which can be considered as the exact and complete expression of his conviction. After he had upset the country with imperturbable coolness, people persuaded themselves that he had acted in virtue of a fixed doctrine. His printed works were searched, and his manuscripts, and the recollections of his conversations, for a series of axioms, wherein they were determined to find the principle of his actions; but this work having been performed with more or less care and intelligence, and from different points of view, the only result is a great deal of obscurity as to the doctrines of the Scotch financier.

We should, perhaps, be liable to give a false idea of Law's genius were we to recommence here the analysis of his writings.

Law was not a man of theory—he was a quack. With an active mind, ingenious, and gifted with rare powers of observation and perception, he had a glimpse of many of the phenomena which have been explained, and systemised more lately by masters of political economy; but he never prided himself on that disinterested curiosity, and that passion for abstract truth which characterise philosophy. His writings were never anything beyond memoranda in support of the business which he wished to set afloat; in practice he never made any scruple of acting in contradiction to his principles. In a word, Law was, in a high order, and with the superiority of an incontestable genius, what is called in every country in the commercial world) a *doer*.

Such men don't discuss scientifically. You must see them at work, and judge of their actions.

CHAPTER III

THE BANK

CHAPTER III

THE BANK

The First French Bank—its Statutes—its Commercial Character

Let us carry ourselves back again to those days of distress and stupor which followed the death of Louis XIV. It was officially announced that the kingdom was exhausted, and that the engagements contracted during the past reign exceeded the resources of the nation; the most rigorous expedients appeared so irresistible that many people considered them legitimate. In the midst of the public consternation a sort of inspired person, a foreigner, suspected for more than one cause, went about declaring everywhere that the violent remedies proposed—bankruptcy, reduction of credit, alteration of the coinage, the Chamber of Justice, arbitrary taxation—would have no other effect than to increase the evil, and that he alone possessed the means of liberating the State and relieving commerce, without injuring any one. Such was the position of Law at his first entrance on a political career. The sympathy of the Regent smoothed the first obstacles. The plans of the reformer were submitted to the

Council on the 24th of October, 1715, less than two months after the death of the King. It was then the question of a Royal Bank carried on by the government, and distributing credit in the name and for the benefit of the State. A majority decided against the project. The firmest of the opponents was the Duke of Saint-Simon, who has thus summed up his opinion in his memoirs: "An establishment of this sort may be good in itself; but it is only so in a republic or in a monarchy like England, whose finances are controlled by those alone who furnish them, and who only furnish so much as they please. But in a State which is weak, changeable, and more than absolute, like France, stability must necessarily be wanting to it; since a King, or in his name a mistress, a minister or favorites, or still more, such extreme necessities as we find in the years 1707 to 1710, may overthrow the Bank—the temptation to which would be too great, and at the same time too easy."

Great convictions are tempered by difficulties. Law immediately put his notion into a new shape. Instead of a public institution he proposed to establish only a private Bank, provided with a capital raised by subscriptions, under the direction of the principal shareholders, and superintended by a committee chosen from amongst the highest Magistrates. He even went so far as to offer to hand over 500,000 livres of his own money to be distributed among the poor, if the success were not equal to his promises.

The formal consent of the Regent and the intrigues of Dubois who, in his way, protected Law, at length triumphed over routine and precautions. Letters patent, dated the 2nd of May, 1716, and registered by Parliament on the 23rd of the same month, authorised the foundation of a *General Bank*.

This establishment was immediately formed with a capital of six millions, divided into 1,200 shares of 5,000 livres, payable in four installments—a fourth part in specie, and three-fourths in State Notes. All regulations were to be decided on by a general meeting of the shareholders, each of whom possessed one vote for every five shares he held. The statutes of the Bank only authorised it to issue notes payable at sight, and to the bearer; to discount commercial paper and bills of exchange, and to receive, on deposit, money of private individuals; to make payments, minus a very small commission, and give receipts for merchants, either in money or by transfer of account; to supply, at the current rate of exchange, bills payable at sight on the managers of the mint in the French provinces, or on the principal bankers of foreign countries.

The Regent having let it be understood that it would please him to see people joining the enterprise, the shares were soon all subscribed for. It is probable that Law himself was the first who took them to a very large amount. By the end of the month of May, the offices engaged at the Hotel de Mesme, in the Rue Sainte-Avoie, were open to the public.

Services Rendered

If the Bank had been founded with resources imposing enough to give offence to the old financial powers, they had not failed to shackle it also. It was its good fortune to excite, at starting, only ridicule and contempt. Could it be otherwise? The first installment of 1,500,000 livers had been effected with only a fourth part in specie, and three-fourths in a depreciated paper, which could not have been realised, perhaps, at a discount of 70 to 80 percent. The disposable cash in hand therefore was reduced to 375,000 livres. With such a capital, a foreigner undertook to establish credit and restore commerce. People thought him mad, and let him have his way.

There were always some elements of success perceived by Law with that quick glance which constituted his strength. The greatest obstacle to the recommencement of business was the continual alteration of the coinage. How could people deal on credit when they had to fear being paid in a depreciated money, worth 20 or 30 percent less than the price agreed on? After the example of the practice at Amsterdam, it was stipulated on Law's Banknotes, that the receipts and payments should be made according to the weight and standard of the day of their issue—that is to say, that silver being at forty livres the marc on the day of the issue of a note, it should be payable at the rate of forty livres the marc whatever might afterwards be the intrinsic value of the coin. In this way, bargains concluded in Bank money entailed no chances which might ruin buyer or seller. The private gentleman who deposited in the Bank a sum representing one hundred marcs of pure silver, was certain to withdraw, whenever he pleased, one hundred marcs of pure silver—a security he would not have had with a notary. Punctuality in payment of the notes on presentation, and in restoring the deposits on the first demand, the advantage of settling the largest transactions with out removal of deposits, and almost without expense, by simple transfers in writing, and above all, the confidence of foreigners, who would only deal on terms of *Bank value*, forcibly struck the public opinion. From an exaggerated distrust, people passed suddenly into a sort of infatuation. Every man of business wished to have his account at the Bank. The demand for its paper against specie was so great, that notes were no longer issued except at a premium.

The rigorous measures taken against the capitalists had left the field open to usury. The best bills were only discounted at 30 percent, or rather at 2 and one-half percent per month, for the paper was at a very short date. In his dealings with trade, Law showed himself less a banker than a statesman. At first starting, he declared that he would take good commercial securities at 6 percent per annum. Scarcely did he perceive that voluntary deposits swelled his floating capital, than he lowered the discount to 4 percent. In a short time he could scarcely register in his books all the discountable securities. Exalted by his success, he exercised a protecting influence over commercial affairs altogether: he anticipated their wants: he offered the support of his credit to establishments whose prosperity seemed an affair of public interest. He revived labour, prevented bankruptcies, advised and encouraged; and, thanks to him, trade, which every one had thought dead, began to show signs of life.

This happened, let us note well, while the Chamber of Justice, by extortion and violence, tended to put capital to flight, and to paralyse trade by terror. A contrast so advantageous to the Scotchman, necessarily raised him highly in public opinion.

An extraordinary favour granted to the Bank considerably augmented its credit. A decree of the Council of State, dated the 10th of April, 1717, commanded all the accountable agents entrusted with the management of the royal revenues, to receive the Banknotes as money in payment of all contributions, and to cash at sight, and without discount, such notes of the said Bank as should be presented to them to the extent of the funds they might have in hand. Thus the innumerable finance-offices became so many branches of the Parisian Bank; the certainty of payment at sight gave an extended currency to the notes. This mysterious connection between a private establishment and the public exchequer, and the increasing influence of Law over the Regent, foretold some hazardous attempt, some project tending to throw power into the hands of the foreigner. Men who felt themselves called on to guide the country took the alarm. A cabal was secretly formed to destroy the Scotchman.

The Envious

The Regent, completely fascinated by Law, had reached that degree of conviction when every contradiction is unbearable.

He thought to crush all resistance at a blow, by uniting the seals of office and the finances in the hands of a man whom he had attached to his own fate by secret bonds, and whom he looked on as his condemned soul. In January, 1718, the lieutenant of police, d'Argenson, replaced d'Aguesseau as vice-chancellor, and the Duke de Noailles, as chief of the finance council. It was natural to imagine that d'Argenson, having till then no pretensions to be called a financier, would accept the full responsibility of the measures concocted by Law and the Regent. The part they intended for him was to carry into execution, as minister of finance, and affix his seal as chief of the magistracy, to their measures.

The Regent had misunderstood the character of d'Argenson. Terrible in his relations with the multitude, supple and officious to the great, mixed up, for twenty years, with strife and intrigue, the lieutenant of police fully enjoyed the reputation of a man of ability: he was proud of it; and for him to accept the two first offices in the State on condition of doing nothing, was to decline grievously. Trembling lest people should suspect the secret of his advancement, he invented a part for himself as painful as it was ridiculous: it was that of a minister bending under the weight of business, but still sacrificing himself for the public good. He was to be seen immersed in an ocean of papers, or dictating to four secretaries at a time. He affected to choose all hours of the night for his appointments, taking care to go and sleep during the day in his private house. In the evening he traversed the streets with a lighted torch in his carriage, to show the people that he was not a moment without working. In actual truth, this laborious minister was neither consulted nor listened to. It is easy to conceive what a frightful rancour must have accumulated in the heart of a man like d'Argenson against the favourite, who condemned him to so ungrateful a part.

D'Argenson secretly lent his assistance to the plots formed

against Law in the administration, in Parliament, and among the men of the old finance. Meanwhile the director of the Bank pursued his experiments. He astonished the public by giving large dividends to the shareholders on a capital of which they supplied but a very small part, and the complete installment of which part was not asked for. What they especially admired was that combination which, allowing the shares to be paid for three-fourths in State Notes, had made these almost worthless securities once more flourishing. Other holders of these notes earnestly begged the ingenious foreigner to invent some new enterprise to render useful a still further sum of this depreciated paper. Amongst other things tending to this object, it was proposed to him to undertake again, at fresh cost, the colonisation of Louisiana, by forming a company with the modest capital of two millions.

Louisiana

What was then called Louisiana was not only the territory which now forms the state of that name, but the immeasurable surface, watered by the Mississippi and its numerous tributaries. Towards the east and west, its extent was without boundary: on the north it extended to the French establishments in Canada. France had taken possession of these deserts for thirty years, when in 1712, a merchant having been so fortunate in his maritime speculations as to gain forty millions by them, Antoine Crozat allowed himself to be seduced by the idea of fertilising a new world. He bought of Louis XIV the grant of Louisiana, with the exclusive right of trading to it for sixteen years. But after five years of attempts and sacrifices, Crozat lost courage; it was then that the idea was suggested to him of giving up his privileges to the able founder of the Bank.

The thing was so little attractive, that the proposal was generally considered as a snare laid for the Scotchman's vanity.

Every one expected a refusal. Law surprised everybody, friends and enemies. He declared that it would be necessary to create not a wretched little shopping affair, existing on a capital of two millions, but a sovereign company fit to rival the great companies of Holland and England, and depending on a capital of one hundred millions, divided into shares of five hundred francs, payable in State Notes. These notes, be it observed, were then at a depreciation of 70 percent: the actual payment, therefore, for a share of five hundred francs would be equal to only one hundred and fifty francs. Law saw no inconvenience in this deficit; and provided, he said, the 4 percent interest on the State Notes were faithfully paid by the Exchequer, he undertook not only to absorb one hundred millions of these in his enterprise, but to raise the remainder of that paper to par. This kind of boasting was repeated all over Paris. People cried out, with one voice, that "if the foreigner performed his promise, he would deserve that France should raise statues to him."

The Western Company

The formation of a "Western Company," intended to cultivate the French possessions in North America, was then resolved on. Letters patent, dated the end of August, 1717, prove the importance that government attached to this undertaking. The only burden imposed on the Company was to render fidelity and homage to the King of France in token of vassalage. The privileges conferred on it, which were to endure for twenty-four years from January, 1718, were the monopoly of all possible trade, comprising the sale of Canadian furs; the perpetual and irrevocable grant of all lands, water-courses, mines, forests, and islands, dependent on Louisiana; the right of selling, alienating, and cultivating these properties, without paying any rent to the mother country; and the right of arming and equipping, in wartime, as many vessels as should be considered necessary for the protection of its commerce. The colonists were exempted from all taxes injurious to the expansion of a new settlement. It was further declared, that the State Notes supplied to form the capital, should be converted into perpetual annuities, the interest of which should be punctually paid at the rate of 25 percent. The purchase of five shares gave one vote in the meetings: foreigners were not forbidden to take shares in the enterprise. Finally, any one could become a shareholder without detracting from his rank or titles.

Although there, were, in these privileges, the elements of a magnificent prospectus, Law was in no haste to launch the enterprise. He had a presentiment of a storm coming. He kept under shelter meanwhile.

The interesting affair, as far as the public was concerned, was the extinction of the State Notes, or what we should now call the payment of the floating debt. Law promised to absorb two-fifths of these notes by employing them in the Western Company. Jealous of the popularity which was the reward of such a service, d'Argenson undertook to extinguish the whole debt at one stroke. He invented nothing better for this purpose than to profit by depreciating the coinage.

A decree of the 10th of May, 1718, raised the price of the silver marc from forty to sixty livres. The minister having procured some ingots at a low price, by means of the merchants of Saint Malo, had them coined at the rate of sixty livres the marc. According to the terms of the decree, it was necessary to bring forty-eight livres in specie, weighing nine ounces and a half, and twelve livres in State Notes, to receive sixty livres of the new coinage, which weighed only eight ounces, so that in reality the capitalist lost by this exchange the sixth part of his specie, and the whole of his paper: it was thus that the State, at that period, paid its debts. We have already spoken, in the first chapter, of the just irritation excited by this decree. The enemies of the Regent thought they had found a pretext for a civil war, and it was a miracle that it did not burst forth.

Forfeiture of the Parliament

Law's enemies, beginning, perhaps, with d'Argenson, had publicly insinuated that the Scotchman was the instigator of the measure which had set the country in a blaze, and that the debasement of the coinage connected itself in his mind with a plan to make the use of paper prevalent. Once launched against authority, the Parliament was on its guard against financial innovations. Daring to overrule the royal edict, which had declared the bank paper admissible for payment of taxes, it forbade all officers of finance to receive the notes in future, and, especially, to discount them with the funds entrusted to them. It renewed, at the same time, the old ordinances which forbade foreigners, under the severest penalties, from interfering in the management of the royal revenue. Lastly, it went so far as to issue a personal summons against Law.

The Bank and its founder could only be saved by a *coup d'etat*. The Regent did not hesitate. He ordered a Bed of Justice to be held, whither the Parliament had to proceed, to the number of sixty-nine members, on foot, and in red robes. After a bitter address from d'Argenson, the King (he was eight years old) handed letters patent, in which was read:—"By our special favour, full power, and royal authority, we have declared, appointed, and ordained, and by these presents signed by our hand, do declare, appoint, ordain, will, and our pleasure is as follows"—that is to say, that the Parliament of Paris shall preserve the right of making remonstrances only on the edicts which shall be submitted to it, and that within eight days; that, in default of any remonstrances within such time, the acts shall be considered as duly registered. This declaration, which a child let fall from the throne, was nothing less than a political revolution. Parliament lost the right of free intervention in affairs of general interest. It fell, properly speaking, under the most absolute despotism.

The Brothers Paris, and the *Anti-Scheme*

D'Argenson triumphed by the defeat of the Parliament, which he detested; but one grief remained to him—that Law shared his victory. He was advised to ruin the popularity of the foreigner, by patronising some speculation brilliant enough to eclipse the Bank and the Western Company.

The most earnest of those who gave this advice to the Keeper of the Seals, were the four brothers Paris, sons of a poor tavern-keeper of Dauphiné. Very meanly employed, about the year 1702, in the transport of provisions intended for the army of Italy, they had contributed, by their zeal, to the success of the Duke de Vendôme's operations. Brought into notice by the report of this service, they had, in their turn become purveyors, great capitalists, and very influential persons, not only by their undoubted cleverness, but by a reputation perhaps superior to their real merits. Government had given them a proof of its confidence by entrusting them with the direction of the *Visa* (or inspection) of 1715. The Chamber of Justice had not dared to proceed against them, and they were still purveyors-general of provisions. In this position Law's renown was distasteful to them; but they knew no other way of combating it than by copying him.

The operation which they planned in secret with d'Argenson consisted in reviving depreciated securities, and employing them as an associated capital in some great enterprise. As it was a custom for the minister of finance to receive a perquisite of 100,000 crowns every time he renewed the leases of the farmers-general of revenues, it was seldom that a minister, on his accession to office, did not find means of rescinding the old contract to make a new one. The farmers lent themselves to the manoeuvre so as to secure the good will of those in power. D'Argenson, therefore, being inclined to renew the leases, the brothers Paris conceived the idea of forming a farming company with a capital of one hundred millions, divided into 100,000 shares of 1,000 francs, payable in annuity contracts, or in notes of the different public treasuries—securities which were at almost as great a depreciation as the State Notes. This company, tendering to the extent of forty-eight millions a year, offered, as a guarantee of its proper management, the one hundred millions of securities, which the State could not refuse, since they emanated from it. The profits were to be divided among the shareholders in proportion to each one's investments. The minister, who was the soul of the whole plot, granted the lease to his valet-de-chamber, Aimon Lambert, the accredited agent of the brothers Paris.

This undertaking is what contemporaries called the *Anti-Scheme*, in opposition to the projects of Law. It was in reality a dangerous rival. The profits to be derived, by making the most of the taxes, were very differently secured from those which could be got out of the marshes of the Mississippi. The brothers Paris were able men, known to deal cautiously: they would try hard to derive one hundred millions from farms obtained at forty-eight millions, so that, deducting all expenses, the profit would probably have been two hundred millions for the six years. But this undertaking, so brilliant for the shareholders, would have been disastrous to the country. Law, on the contrary, like a true artist in finance, and a disinterested artist, always associated the State with his enterprises. Besides, the economical position of the country was not much improved; and, in spite of the most unfortunate remedies, a crisis was always imminent. The fortunate founder of the Bank promised to regenerate the country. Was it not natural to ward off intrigues and rivalries, and to leave the field open for his labours? This resolution was taken, in the conferences which were held towards the end of the year 1718, between the Regent, the Duke de Bourbon, the Duke d'Antin, and Law. It is from this period that the series of financial adventures commence, which contemporaries called the *Scheme*.

CHAPTER IV

THE SCHEME

CHAPTER IV

THE SCHEME

The Royal Bank

On the 4th of December, 1718, a proclamation of the King, converted the General Bank into a *Royal Bank*, from the 1st January, 1719. "This was," says an excellent judge,[1] "to take away from its engagements the limited, but real, guarantee of an actual capital, to substitute in its place the indefinite but doubtful guarantee of an indebted State." To effect this change, the State brought up the 1,200 shares of which the first capital had been formed. On these shares of 5,000 livres, only the first fourth had been paid—namely 375 livres in specie, and 1,125 livres in bad paper, whose value at the current rate was not more than 400 livres at the most. The reimbursement was made at par and in silver, so that the shareholders who had advanced less than 800 livres received 5,000. Never had investment been more profitable.

With the afterthought of forming a reserved capital for

---

1. M. Gantier, deputy-governor of the Bank of France.

the purpose of feeding the whole concern, it became very difficult to retain the clause which had made the fortune of the Bank—that which consisted in paying in specie according to the legal coinage current at the time of its establishment. One hundred livres at the rate of silver in 1719 (that is to say, sixty livres to the marc) would have equalled only ninety francs of our time, while the same sum in Bank money (that is to say, at forty livres the marc) would have represented 135 francs. A proportionate calculation was necessary on each issue of notes. It would clearly have been impossible to popularise the use of paper on these conditions. It was therefore decreed that the Bank money should in future consist of "*livres tournois* of a fixed and unvarying value, whatever might be the future variations of coined money."

This change raised a presentiment unfavourable to the new establishment among men of good sense. To keep up paper at the expense of silver, a fixed value was given to the former, while insinuating that the latter might be tampered with arbitrarily. Besides, the promissory note could only have a relative value to the sum it represented in silver. Pretending to fix the price of paper, while modifying the natural price of the precious metals, is nonsense.

Credit is only established on conviction, and only subsists on liberty. Law was more persuaded of this than any other man; and nevertheless surrounded by enemies, and obliged to satisfy the impatience of the spoilt children which absolute princes almost always produce, he entered, in spite of himself, upon that fatal course in which he could only maintain his position by arbitrary acts and abuse of power—it was walking to destruction. A new decree of the council constituted, in several large towns, branches of the Bank with two funds—one to cash at sight the notes, and the other to receive the specie offered in exchange for the notes.[2] The same edict commanded that, in the places where such branches were established, silver money should not be tendered in payment of a less sum than 600 livres, the remainder being obliged to be paid in notes; and that even for a less sum the notes should not be refused. The directors of the messageries, or transport offices, were forbidden to convey gold and silver to the towns of the Branch Banks except on account, and with the authority of the Bank. On the whole the proceeding was not so very threatening, since the person paid in notes had only to take them at once to the Bank and convert them into coin. It was only an attempt to make credit securities grow with common use. But this attempt against liberty was not the less a bad omen: it was even a blunder in a commercial point of view. It is most likely that a great many more notes would be presented for change than if the circulation had been perfectly free.

Stock Jobbing Lessons

The high reputation which Law needed for his vast projects depended much upon the performance of his promise, publicly made, to raise the value of, and sustain at par, the State Notes. A powerful stroke of some kind was needed, but it was at hand. The business of the Western Company had been at a standstill for a year. The shares were allotted, because they were to be paid for in paper which nobody knew what to do with: but there they remained through the rivalry of the *Anti-Scheme* and the intrigues of the brothers Paris. Suddenly Law gave an irresistible impulse to the rise by purchasing at par, at six months' date, and even at a premium of 30 to 40 percent, shares, which were

---

2. This experiment was only tried in Lyons, la Rochelle, Tours, Orleans, and Amiens. They were afraid of establishing offices of this kind in the Parliament towns, where hostile manifestations were to be feared.

then at a depreciation of one-half; that is to say, he offered to pay one hundred livres in six months' date for a share, of which the current price was fifty livres, giving thirty to forty livres earnest into the bargain. This was acting not like a prudent financier, but like a wild gambler. Nevertheless, this very excess of daring among a people inexperienced in stockjobbing, was a mark of ability. The shares rose to par. Law was beginning to be, in the eyes of the public, a kind of magician wielding a mysterious power.

The director of the Bank, in concealing his own game while he saw that of his adversaries, played a safe card. His apparent rashness was to procure him large profits. Supported by the government, whose movements he directed, he took measures to unite the Western Company with other commercial companies. It was clear that, by accumulating the chances of profit, he would end by raising the shares to par, and even above it.

The Indian Company.

Following the successful example given by other commercial countries, France tried for more than a century to establish privileged companies to cultivate distant lands. Besides the Western Company, which Law had first created by uniting Crozat's grant with the monopoly of selling beaver, there was also a *Guinea Company* working the West Coast of Africa, with the view of a traffic in Negroes. As for a monopoly of trade of the East, it belonged to an old Company reconstituted by Colbert in 1664. There was also a private privilege granted in 1713 for the China trade, but not yet worked. By uniting these enterprises to the new Western Company, Law was about to mass together in his own hands the entire foreign trade.

The fusion, therefore, of the Companies then existing, more or less flourishing, composed the new *Indian Company*. The decree which founds it, is dated in the month of May, 1719. To the monopolies and favours already conceded to the Company of which Law was the patron, letters patent added the sole privilege of trading from Guinea to the Japanese Archipelago, of colonising especially the Cape of Good Hope, the East Coast of Africa, that which is washed by the Red Sea, all the known islands on the Pacific, Persia, the Mogul Empire, the kingdom of Siam, China, Japan, and South America. The concession carried with it the exclusive right of importing from these countries all products, natural or manufactured, not prohibited in France, with facilities for selling the prohibited articles to foreign countries. Favoured by premiums and exemption from taxes, the new Company was declared proprietor of the lands, fortresses, dwellings, warehouses, moveable and immoveable property, credits, vessels, supplies of war, provisions; in a word, everything which had composed the property of the preceding Companies.

These brilliant enumerations were addressed to an ignorant multitude. Men of experience knew what to expect from an Eastern trade. The company founded by Colbert had only been kept in foot for forty years, because, during the most unfortunate affairs, there were always some people interested in prolonging its existence. The directors alone derived profit from it: there was nothing but valueless shares for the shareholders. The magic ability of Law was reckoned on to resuscitate the enterprise; but taking things at their best, the dividends to be shared were so far off, that they could have no influence on the present price of shares.

The Mississippi

On the other hand, the countries watered by the Mississippi, immense, unknown virgin solitudes, which the imagination might people with treasures, were an unlimited field open to quackery. Public credulity was practised on with rare impudence.

From the outset the art of "puffing" was carried to its utmost limits. Large engravings were circulated representing the arrival of the French at the Missisippi, and showing, in the midst of an enchanting country, male and female savages running to meet their new masters with every demonstration of respect and admiration. "There are seen," said the accompanying description, "mountains full of gold and silver, copper, lead, and quicksilver. As these metals are very common, and the savages know nothing of their value, they exchange lumps of gold and silver for European manufactures, such as knives, cooking utensils, spindles, a small looking-glass, or even a little brandy." One episode in the engravings was addressed to pious folks: savages were seen falling at the feet of their reverences the Jesuits, and the inscription said:—"The idolatrous Indians earnestly pray that they may receive baptism. Great care is taken of the education of their children."

There was among the people an old soldier named Lamothe Cadillac, formerly employed in Louisiana, of which he did not retain a very agreeable recollection. He had the imprudence to say that the wonders attributed to this country were so many fables. The simplicity of this man might become dangerous, so they made sure of his discretion by sending him to the Bastille.

Whilst the *Scheme* lasted they took care to keep up the enthusiasm to a fitting height, by issuing pompous advertisements about it, announcing the departure of a fleet laden with merchandise for different parts of the world, or the return of vessels with millions. At one time they talked of a manufactory of 1,200 Indian women engaged in making silk. At another, they announced that ingots of silver found at the Mississippi were going to be assayed at the mint. At a time when jewels were much in fashion, it was declared that a rock of emerald existed in Arkansas, and that Captain de Laharpe had been sent with a detachment of twenty-two men to take possession of it.

To tell the truth, the Mississippi was then only a scarcely habitable desert, desolated by fevers in its lower part, and terrible from the savages in its higher regions. There were only four or five hundred whites and twenty blacks in all Louisiana when Crozat made over the viceroyalty of it to the Western Company. In point of establishments everything was to be done. After the year 1718, Law sent out workmen under the direction of the engineer, Delatour, and laid the foundation of a town to which he gave the name of his patron: such was the origin of New Orleans. In France, the Company purchased Belle Isle on the sea, to make a depot of it, and built the pretty fort of Lorient, which has now become an important place: but these creations were expenses without profit. The true wealth of the new world, agriculture, having been neglected for a chimerical secret for gold and silver, and precious stones, trade declined for want of nourishment.

"Daughters" and "Grand-daughters."

The shares of the Western Company, purchased by State Notes which could not be realised, had supplied no capital for working. In founding the Indian Company by the union of all the monopolies granted to the foreign trade, Law was authorised to issue 50,000 new shares of 500 francs each, payable in specie, and by twentieths, monthly, with a discount of fifty francs on paying in full at the time of allotment. This combination placed in the hands of the daring director a sum of 27,500,000 francs in silver. Disturbed by all these novelties which it could scarcely understand, Parliament refused its consent: this circumstance retarded the enforcement of the edict for about six weeks. In the interval the original shares purchased with State Notes rose to 130. A fifth only of these shares had been paid for; so that he who had advanced one hundred livres in bad paper, could already receive for it 630 livres in crown-pieces.

Law's promise was already more than performed: but that was nothing. He caused a new decree (of the 20th of June) in which it was said that, in consequence of the high value of the shares recently issued, it was just to establish a general rule which should be susceptible of no favour: that, consequently, no one should be allowed to take up these new shares without possessing a sum of old shares four times larger than that for which he now wished to subscribe. Thus, to obtain ten shares of the second series, it was necessary to possess forty of the first. The public called the latter *Mothers*, and the others, *Daughters*. Each of these *daughters* brought her dowry with her: when you had obtained her by means of 550 livres, you could immediately derive from her, from hand to hand, a profit which doubled and tripled the investment. Let any one judge of the number of suitors!

"It is easy to conceive," says Forbonnais, "the favour which this rule gave to the shares of the Western Company, and it was carried to excess by the haste with which the new shares were taken up. It is even asserted that the author of the *Scheme* contributed to this policy by secret agents, so as to double the enthusiasm. When no more *daughters* were to be found, the Western shares were sought for at any price. They were bought for ready money, or on credit, with a premium on the price agreed on. Some sold so as to make sure of a large profit, and then, seeing that the shares still went up, bought again. In such a state of fermentation, the quickness of the transactions did not admit of the employment of coin: the note was preferred to it; and so that the public might not want that, they did not put too high a price on it."

The Company had the art of fostering the enthusiasm, by adding, every now and then, a new branch of operations to its domains. In the course of the year 1719, they thus managed to get the monopoly of tobacco at a price of 4,020,000 livres. They farmed the salt mines of Alsace and Franche-Compté. They offered to pay the pensions and other debts of the State, minus a discount of 3 percent. A little later they undertook the collection of taxes gathered directly by the Exchequer, reimbursing the offices of the receivers-general. All these enterprises, successively adding new revenues to the already known resources, were chronicled forth in a manner calculated to sustain the rise.

In the opinions current at that time, the right of making a profit out of the coining of money was one of the resources of the Crown. By Law's intervention the profit of the coinage was made over to the Company for nine years, minus a sum of fifty millions, to be paid by it to the King in fifteen consecutive months. This new source of profit, which was exaggerated, immediately raised the price of the shares to 1,000 livres. At present the *Scheme* was only at its outset, and yet the profits already reached 100 percent.

To get together the capital of fifty millions promised to the State, it became necessary to create new shares. A decree of the council authorised the Company to issue 50,000, which, at the nominal price of 500 livres, would only have produced twenty-five millions. But it would have been too generous to give shares at par, which rose immediately cent percent. Thinking to profit by this premium, the Company gave notice that it would allot, at the rate of 1,000 livres, these new shares of 500 livres. Even to obtain them at that price it was necessary to hold old shares for a sum five times as large, and then to pay for them, not in coin, but in bank paper. These obstacles excited the imagination and whetted desire. The new shares, which were called *granddaughters*, were sought after as eagerly as the *daughters*, and made their *mothers* worth so much the more. The rise on the shares of the Indian Company reached 200 percent. The State Notes, and all the depreciated paper of the former reign, obeyed the same impulse, and rose to par.

Paying off the Annuities

About the beginning of September, a new series of operations crowned the *Scheme*. The Indian Company, or rather Law, who was the soul of it, offered to take on lease the farms of the revenues granted the previous year to Aimon Lambert, and to lend to the King, at 3 percent, a sum of 1,200 millions to pay off the different creditors of the State. This combination was doubly seductive to Law. In destroying the lease which the brothers Paris had obtained in the name of Aimon Lambert, he overthrew the *Anti-Scheme*, and took a cruel vengeance on his enemies. In paying off the debts of the State he gloriously realised what was then the ideal of financiers.

The offer of the Indian Company, long ago settled in the secret councils of the Regency, was officially accepted on the 2nd of September. The minister of finance, d'Argenson, who, we are assured, was never consulted, was obliged to cancel the brilliant affair with which he had gratified his *valet de chambre*, an affront which drove into fury his concentrated hatred. The Indian Company, on taking up the lease for nine years, consented to an augmentation of two and one-half millions, which raised it to fifty-two millions. To realise the 1,200 millions, which it offered to pay the King, it was authorised to issue shares to the bearer, conferring a right to eventual profits, or contracts for annuities at 3 percent, payable half yearly, from the 1st of January, 1720. The due payment of this annuity was guaranteed by the interest of the sum advanced to the State. Thus, on the one hand, the Company borrowed at 3 percent, and on the other it lent at 3 percent. The affair was only a sort of conversion of annuities, which, by transferring the debt of the public exchequer to a private company, allowed the State to diminish by 35 millions, the interest with which it was chargeable.

It was wished to extinguish, together with the annuities, what remained of the State Notes, and other paper bearing interest. These operations brought with them the suppression of many expenses and offices; moreover, it was necessary to reimburse the one hundred millions lately paid by the shareholders of the *Anti-Scheme* since the lease had been annulled, the presumed profit of which guaranteed the interest of their capital. The sum of 1,200 millions, first intended for the extinction of these debts, having proved insufficient, the Company raised its offers to 1,500 millions, in consideration of which the privileges of every kind which had been previously granted to it were confirmed for fifty years.

Organization of the Company—its Balance Sheet

The work began almost at once. Government delivered to its creditors orders on the cashier of the Indian Company. On its part, the Company created, in four issues, 324,000 new shares, at a nominal price of 500 livres, reserving for itself the right of profiting by the premium which was then at 1,000 percent, so that the 324,000 shares would give it a sum of 1,620 millions.

To give renown to the enterprise, it was installed in a manner suited to its high destiny. The Company purchased that part of the old Mazarin Palace, which at present contains the engravings and manuscripts of the National Library, and it extended from both sides of the Rue Vivienne by the purchase of six large houses. The Bank, first established in the Rue Sainte-Avoie, was transferred to the buildings which abut on the Rue Vivienne. The hotel and the offices of the Indian Company, back-to-back to the Bank, were entered by the Rue de Richelieu. The Council of Administration was composed of thirty directors, chosen as much as possible from among the old farmers-general of revenue, and in the number of whom Law figured without any apparent distinction. A security was required of them of 500,000 livres, the interest of which was paid to them; their salaries did not exceed 10,000 livres. The programme of their labours gives an idea of overwhelming activity. The inferior officials were selected by Law from that obscure crowd among which so many men of merit are always struggling. The accounts were excellent while entrusted to simple clerks: disorder was introduced later by official personages whom favour thrust among them.

Everyone could now understand in what consisted that which was called the *Scheme*. A colossal immense Company tending to become the sole merchant and financier, provided with monopolies sufficiently rich to intoxicate the imagination by the hope of considerable gain, managed to make the annuitants wish to get rid of their annuities to enter into an affair from which they expected wonders. In theory, this conception was admirable. It would even be advantageous for a country that the annuities, instead of being founded on the State, that is to say, instead of being an unproductive burthen on the taxes, should spring from the natural productions of a profitable speculation. But was the conception of Law of a nature to realise this ideal? We shall judge by the general plan of the undertaking.

On the following page is a table setting out the number and value of the shares Issued by the Indian Company.

Number and Value of the Shares Issued by the Indian Company

Successive emissions	Number of shares	Nominal price of shares	Total price	Actual price per share	Actual price of each emission
1st Capital	200,000	500	100,000,000	500	100,000,000
1st Subscription	50,000	500	25,000,000	500	27,500,000
2nd Subscription	50,000	500	25,000,000	1,000	50,000,000
3rd Subscription	300,000	500	150,000,000	5,000	1,500,000,000
Supplementary	24,000	500	12,000,000	5,000	120,000,000
	624,000		312,000,000		1,797,500,000

Thus, the Company had issued 624,000 shares of 500 livres each, representing 312 millions of livres; but, profiting by the rise, it had sold them for 1,797,500,000 livres.

Now let us see on what it reckoned to pay the dividends of this enormous sum:

livres

Interest of 3 percent due by the State, to deduct from the lease of the farms,	48,600,000
Profit of the Company on the said lease,	8,000,000
Monopoly of tobacco,	6,000,000
Profits on direct receipts, the Salt Mines, etc.,	1,400,000
Profits on the Coinage,	10,000,000
Revenues of the Company's commercial privileges,	8,000,000
Net total of probable receipts	82,000,000

At this rate the Company might have paid a dividend of 130 livres per share of 500 livres, a magnificent result in ordinary circumstances. But here, let us remark, the greatest part of the subscribers had bought their shares not at 500, but 5,000 livres;

and, in order that these should receive a dividend of even 4 percent, it would have been necessary that the dividend on each share should amount to 200 livres.

Law seriously reckoned on such a progress. In his erroneous theory on the production of wealth, he made the enrichment of a country depend on the disposable cash. Besides, having proved that the share scrip, payable to bearer, circulating from hand to hand, passed as money, he was persuaded that the unlimited rise of the shares increasing the national capital, would bring about so great a prosperity that the Company could increase its profits, and give a dividend of at least 200 livres per share. Instead of moderating the Stockjobbing fever, he over-excited it by all kinds of manoeuvres. This error brought on the strange mania to which he owes his celebrity.

CHAPTER V

THE GOLDEN AGE

CHAPTER V

THE GOLDEN AGE

The Rue Vivienne

Up to the month of September, 1719, the allotment of the Company's shares was conducted with an appearance of order. To obtain them, it was necessary to fulfill certain conditions. Another plan was adopted to get rid of the 324,000 shares offered at 5,000 livres: they were sold by auction, and everybody might aspire to them. It is easy to imagine the eagerness, the plots, the passionate rage of the multitude, bent on securing this magic paper whose price rose every hour to such an extent that people were met with rich and triumphing in the evening, who had been needy and embarrassed in the morning.

The scrip was issued in series, according to the wants of the place. The delivery took place at the Company's Hotel. As soon as a new distribution was announced, the Rue Vivienne and the adjacent streets were filled with a tumultuous and maddened crowd. The aspirants arrived—some bending under bags of coin, others having their pocketbooks thrust tightly into their bosoms. They fell into rank looking at each other with scowling eyes. "Their phalanx advanced for several days and nights towards the Exchange office, like a compact column, which neither sleep, hunger, nor thirst could destroy. But at the fatal cry which announced the delivery of the last share, the whole vanished at once."[1]

The Rue Quincampoix

As soon as he was provided, each of these birds of prey took his flight to the place called *The Street*; just as the ancients said *the City* to express Rome, the Queen-City. This was the Rue Quincampoix.

The streets Saint-Martin and Saint-Denis appear to have been, in remote times, the scene of considerable trade. Between these two fines were the changers and bankers grouped, having built over land which, in the days of Philip Augustus, was still in cultivation. Along the boundary wall extended the street called *Oues*, that is to say, *Oies* (geese)—thus called because the cooks had taken up their quarters there, near to the folks who gained money and liked to spend it. In time the Rue aux *Oues* became the Rue aux Ours (Bears). The bear began by being a goose: these metamorphoses are common in history.

By closing up and forming in line, the pleasure-houses of the bankers made the Rue Quincampoix, thus called from the name of one of its principal inhabitants. Long custom made it the centre of the trade in paper. He who had to realise a contract of annuity, a bill of exchange, an order on an establishment or a company, went and offered it, in this quarter of the town, from door to door: and as the exchange was made from hand to hand without public control, no doubt a great deal of roguery was committed in it. The trade was very active there during the last years of Louis XIV, on account of the deluge of paper, the only

---

1. Lemontey—History of the Regency

resource of the great King. The best was done at a depreciation of three-fourths. This trade was full of risk, so it was admitted that the money employed in it ought to bring at least 1,000 percent. There was even a class of brokers who, totally destitute of capital, carried on by means of *loans by the clock*, that is to say, that at the moment of concluding the bargain, they rushed off to some Jew in the neighbourhood, who entrusted them with the necessary money at the rate of a quarter percent per quarter of an hour, and sometimes even more.

The Rue Quincampoix was, therefore, perfectly prepared for the scenes of which it became the theatre during the *Scheme*. In 1719, it was a passage of a hundred and fifty feet long by five or six wide, terminating at one end in the Rue aux Ours, and at the other in the Rue Aubry-le-Boucher. To judge of it by the engravings of the time, the houses were then handsomer and more regular than now. The conversion of all public securities into State Notes after the *Visa*, the demand for these State Notes to enter the Western Company, the manoeuvres of the *Anti-Scheme*, and the shares of the Indian Company, altogether gave an accelerated impetus to stockjobbing. While running to the counting houses, people met in the Rue Quincampoix. A custom sprang up of addressing one another there, talking of public affairs, and their influence on the prices of shares. The transactions taking place by the simple exchange of a share, payable to bearer for banknotes or a bag of crown-pieces, were soon accomplished without any intermediate assistance, with extreme celerity, and between people who did not know one another, and might never see one another again.

The increasing concourse of people intercepted the traffic. The determination was then adopted of transforming the street into a kind of exchange, by enclosing it at its two extremities with gates, open for the public from morning till night. They were obliged even to forbid night meetings, on the complaint of the inhabitants of that district, whose sleep was no longer possible. Persons of quality entered by the Rue Aubry-le-Boucher, and the general public by the Rue aux Ours; but all distinction was lost within the sanctuary. Nobles and footmen, bishops and clergy, shopkeepers and workmen, men of the sword and men of the shop, magistrates and pickpockets, marquises and servants, Frenchmen and foreigners, out of breath, shouting, plotting, seizing on the papers, counting the crown-pieces, formed a spectacle in which dramatic frenzy was mingled with outrageous buffoonery.

The fashionable commerce engendered several accessory speculations. The most lucrative was that in lodgings. Well-informed persons, "foreseeing from the commencement that the ground of the street would rise in value to such an extent, that ten square feet might bring in the income of a lordly estate, possessed themselves of all the houses then to let, as well as all the apartments, to sub-let them in parts. This foresight created large fortunes. The offices were let at two, three or four hundred livres the month along the whole extent of the ground, so that a house hired at six or eight hundred livres a year, contained twenty or thirty offices: from whence the profit may be judged of.[2]"

After this example nearly all the private individuals, landlords or tenants, living in the Rue Quincampoix or in the neighbouring streets, divided their dwellings into offices, without even excepting the attics and the cellars. Some sorts of boxes were even seen erected on the roofs. Buvat mentions an attorney of the Châtelet who let out a lower room in his house at the rate of 50 livres a day, which would have amounted to 18,000 livres a year.

The dealers in provisions in the neighbourhood did not know whom to listen to, and gold flowed in heaps. The tavern

---

2. Duhautchamp—History of the Scheme.

keepers, confectioners, and cooks, to rid themselves of the crowd, placed excessive prices on their provisions; but no one thought of bargaining: a partridge put up to a kind of auction in the Rue aux Ours was knocked down at 200 livres. There were some *Cafés* for lords and fine ladies, who, negligently reclining at ease, sipped their coffee and played at quadrille, whilst their brokers came to tell them of the fluctuations on 'Change[3], and to take their orders.

Foreigners in Paris

In the progressive phase of the shares, stockjobbing was a game at which everybody won. The idea that it was sufficient to take part in it to get rich, spreading far and wide, there was a time when all Europe looked to the Rue Quincampoix with longing eyes. At the end of 1719, the number of provincials and foreigners assembled in Paris either to speculate, or from curiosity, was estimated at 500,000. Many sovereigns had their accredited agents there, solely charged with following the trade in shares. To diminish this concourse a decree was issued, according to the terms of which all public functionaries come to speculate, were to depart again on the eighth day, "under pain of being deprived of their offices, the business of which was being neglected, and, as it were, abandoned." Imagine the feverish impatience, the despair of those who were detained at a distance whether they were tied to their duties, or that means of conveyance were wanting to them. We read, on this subject, in Buvat's Journal: "Letters from Lyons, Aix, Bordeaux, Strasbourg, and Brussels, state that the carriages and public conveyances in these places are engaged two months in advance, and people speculate there in the places engaged to come to Paris." Thus for want of shares in the Indian Company,

---

3. The stock exchange.

people speculated in diligence tickets, which were bought at a greater or less premium according as the time of departure was more or less near.

The Parisians

A very characteristic fact has been remarked. In the midst of this polyglot masquerade, where, above all, resounded the accents of English, Dutch, Germans, Swiss, Flemish, people of Languedoc, Lyons, Provence, Dauphiny, Gascony, Normandy, Lorraine, and Franche-Compté, few Parisians were to be met except in the character of merely curious people. The Parisians were not infatuated with the *Scheme* until it began to decline. While it gave profits, they kept to their characters of joking lookers-on, making *bon-mots* and songs about it. Under the title of *Christmas*, a kind of satirical review of men and things was sent forth, in a form and to an air agreed on.

"All the people in France," said the song, "hearing of the birth of the Saviour, betook themselves to Bethlehem, having the chiefs of the State at their head." Each personage, passing in his turn before the manger of the divine infant, is greeted with some epigram, a naïve translation of the popular sentiments regarding them. In the retirement of their own houses in the evening, the good citizens sang these squibs to the jovial air of *"Les Borgeois de la Châtre:"* this opposition within closed doors was the "Journalism" of the time. Law was not forgotten in the *Christmas* of 1719, which has not less than ninety-six couplets. But the accent of anger does not yet vibrate:—

> *With arrogant air*
> *Law appeared in this place;*
> *With an insolent voice*
> *He said to the King of Heaven—*
> *Lord! you are wretchedly poor:*

you're without everything down here;
Take some shares,
Take, take,
And don't neglect
To open an account at the Bank.

People who have attempted to exonerate the author of the *Scheme* from the reproach of having excited the stockjobbing, say that, on the contrary, he made sincere efforts to restrain it; but that he was carried away beyond all bounds by the impetuosity of the French. It is difficult to admit such an excuse. In theory, Law looked upon the unlimited rise of public securities as the ideal of prosperity, and in practice he fostered it by all sorts of means. Not only he set the example of the game of time-bargains, but he facilitated it by making considerable advances in Banknotes on the deposit of shares; so that by the deposit of a single share several others could be purchased for the account.[4] He had the shares of 5,000 livres divided into coupons of 500 livres, equally payable by tenths, so as to popularise the investment. He constantly multiplied the Banknotes, so that there might be no want of capital for these transactions. He tampered with the coinage; he weakened the guarantees, which are inherent in the very nature of the latter, to make paper preferred to real money; and (strangely enough!) he found the secret which philosophers have vainly sought after, of making people despise gold and silver.

Gold and Silver Disdained

A decree of the 26th of September having declared that the shares of the Company could only be paid for in Banknotes, or in the provisional receipts which were given to the paid-off

---

4. The advances of this kind amounted to 450 millions.

annuitants, these securities were immediately quoted at 10 percent premium. "Generally 11,000 livres in gold were given for 10,000 in State-paper; and sufficiently large brokerage was paid to bring little fortunes to those who possessed the secret of effecting these exchanges quickly." The crown-pieces were for the time proscribed in the Rue Quincampoix. "If you have only gold," they used to say, "no bargain." As for silver, no one would have dared to offer it.

A M. de Cambis having gone to the street to sell some shares, addressed himself, from preference, to a man of rank like himself. The affair was soon concluded: but, behold! The purchaser, preparing to pay, drew a bag full of gold from his pocket. The one declared that he had reckoned on paper, and rejected the vile metal; the other declared that no one could refuse the current specie. They grew hot on the subject, drew their swords, and already some passes had been exchanged, when a broker, thrusting himself between the combatants, cried out: "Is it possible that two noblemen should thus risk their precious lives? What remorse you are preparing for the conqueror! Ah! Gentlemen, spare blood so useful to your country,—permit me to arrange between you." And, thereupon, the broker drawing the two champions into his stall, gave them paper in exchange for the gold. This action did so much honour to the industrious and generous individual that history has preserved his name—it is Veron.

Unheard of tricks, employed to influence the funds, brought about unforeseen and terrible fluctuations, impoverishing some, and enriching others from morning until night. Emissaries, in the pay of the great stockjobbers, spread themselves about in the crowd under all sorts of disguises to play their parts learnt beforehand. On agreed signals, such as the stroke of a bell, a whistle, a piece of drapery displayed at a window, they told news, true or false, raised fear or enthusiasm, and offered to buy or to sell at all prices. These barefaced manoeuvres, coinciding with the efforts of an absolute government to create a rise, raised and kept up for a fortnight at 20,000 livres, shares, the nominal value of which was 500 livres. Any one who, during the last months of 1718, had laid out 20,000 livres in specie in purchasing the State Notes which were converted into shares, might have realised two millions in gold at the end of 1719.

The Mississippians

It is not surprising that, in the midst of such robbery, people of ready and unscrupulous character should have acquired extravagant fortunes. The list of Mississippians (such was the name commonly given to enriched shareholders) has preserved the names of more than one hunderd persons who gained, whilst the *Scheme* lasted, above twenty millions each.

A Madame Chaumont, of Namur, came as a party to a law-suit, which threatened her ruin, and gained more than one hundred millions in the Rue Quincampoix. Vincent Leblanc, a rich speculator of old standing, was no less fortunate. André, son of a fellmonger of Montelimont, overwhelmed with debts in 1718, and in such disrepute that one of his creditors had offered bills to the amount of 10,000 livres signed by him for a single breakfast, found himself possessor of seventy millions in 1720. Dupin, a servant of the banker Tourton, retired with fifty millions. A Savoyard, originally an errand-boy and scrub, giving himself the name of Chambery from his birthplace, and following the custom of those who had not even a name of their own, amassed forty millions, and aspired to purchase the place of Secretary to the King, which he could not effect by reason of his origin. A waiter at a tavern, named Gabriel Bourdon, realised thirty millions, went to England, and came back after the *Scheme*, playing in Paris the part of a *Milord* with an equipage and English servants. Less sensible, a certain

Abbé Duval gained eighteen millions, and ruined himself in folly. A moneychanger named Lamothe, provided with twenty millions, took an unfortunate idea into his head of coining, and was sent to the galleys. Several Englishmen, admitted to Law's intimacy, carried away enormous sums from France.

New Occupations

Under this category, in which the profits may be reckoned by the tens of millions, a number of people realised in a few months, gains superior to what a whole lifetime of work and economy could have procured them in their ordinary pursuits. Unexpected fortunes were often the rewards of most trifling services. For instance, "a cobbler who worked under four planks in the Rue Quincampoix, determined to metamorphose his little stall into an office, which he furnished with several stools for ladies to sit on who were drawn to the spot by curiosity. Seeing that this notion succeeded, he abandoned his work to supply pens and paper for the transactions which took place in his shop. This new trade, added to the money given for his seats, was worth 200 livres a day to him in the height of the business."

Many individuals, unable to speculate on their own account, offered the use of paper and pencils, and bent their backs for those who had calculations to make. Among these walking desks some acquired a reputation, either for their good humour or for the convenience that their shapes presented. A little hunchback gained 150,000 livres at this trade. A soldier, with extraordinarily broad shoulders, received small notes enough to enable him to purchase his discharge and retire to a pretty estate. A nobleman, named de Nanthia, lived extremely well by the same occupation, in spite of his noble family.

Many small shopkeepers and workmen left their counters and workshops to turn brokers: it was in this way a great many began who afterwards became capitalists. The changes were so quick and so soon effected that an agent sent on the market to realise 10,000 livres, could easily get 11,000 or 12,000, and profit by the difference, since no trace remained of these transactions carried on between people unknown to each other.

One of the strangest caprices of fortune happened to a man who scarcely deserved it. His name was Dalesne, and he was the son of a councillor in the Parliament of Bordeaux. Without resources in Paris, and after a youth full of wild deeds, he gained the confidence of a banker, who entrusted him with papers from which he was to procure 17,000 livres. Dalesne dealt with the son of a lemonade-seller, at whose house the principal stockjobbers assembled; but the latter, already embroiled with the officers of justice, disappeared without paying him. The banker, suspecting his agent of connivance with the thief, threatened to have him hanged. The affair was so much the more serious to Dalesne, as he had worked under a false name, having been condemned to death at Bordeaux for getting his father assassinated. The Bordeaux gentleman therefore took to flight in despair, and on his road overtook the first fugitive. He again got possession of the papers, returned to Paris, profited by a rise of cent percent which had taken place in an interval of some days, reentered the banker's house in triumphant style, restoring him his 17,000 livres, and still remained possessor himself of a similar sum with which he set to work on his own account. This Dalesne grew rich during the *Scheme*, and died possessing the finest estates in the county of Avignon. His history was only discovered after his death, notwithstanding the town of Bordeaux had erected a pyramid to invoke public execration on the parricide.

A Shower of Gold at Court

An undertaking like that of Law, and in a country such as France then was, needed many and powerful supports. In the midst of those gilded and titled beggars called courtiers, "the author of the *Scheme*," says Saint-Simon, "had a gracious word and a free hand for every one. In his paper he had a financial tap, which he turned on to any one who could support it." He enriched the great folks by teaching them how to manoeuvre in the Rue Quincampoix: he gratified the common herd of nobles by downright gifts. In the great stroke which followed the affair of paying off the annuities, the Duke de Bourbon gained twenty millions, with which he paid his debts, and set himself afloat; and it is declared that the whole of his profits in two years exceeded sixty millions. The Duke d'Antin had twelve millions for his share. The Prince de Conti, whom Law did not admit to his confidence, having only derived 4 and one-half millions, showed his ill-humour, and thenceforth threw himself into an opposition which became very injurious to the *Scheme*. The favorites of the Regent, especially the Marquis de Lassé, the Marshall d'Estreés, and the Duke de Laforce, and Madame de Vérue, made several millions. What Dubois took for himself no one ever knew: he dipped into the treasury at discretion. In short, everybody at Court asked for shares, speculated, gained, and squandered; the rage for amassing and speculating was a sort of contagion which was resisted among the great only by the Chancellor d'Aguesseau, the Marshalls de Villeroy and de Villars, the Dukes of Saint-Simon and of La Rochefoucauld.

That Law, a foreigner at Court, in pursuit of his perfidious machinations, and without any other support than his own ability, should make great sacrifices to gain over a body of supporters, is easy to conceive; but the prodigalities of the Regent are inexcusable. They especially contributed to the discredit of the *Scheme*. What confidence could sensible people feel in those leaves of paper which sprang up under the capricious breath of favour? "We hear nothing but millions spoken of now," says the Princess Palatine, the Regent's mother, in her curious letters; "my son has given me two millions in shares, which I have distributed among my household. The King has also taken some millions for his household. All the royal household have received some, all the children of France, the grandchildren of France, and the Princes of the blood." On the departure for the war in Spain, a large distribution of shares and notes was made among the superior and lower officers. The Regent increased, by 130,000 livres, his mother's pension; he granted a pension of 60,000 livres to the Count de la Marche, a son of the Prince de Conti, scarcely thirteen years old. As if he had at length found out the secret of making gold, which he had sought after in his youth, he no longer knew how to refuse the solicitations of any who asked him for an increase of allowance or pension. Indignant at these disorders, the Duke Saint-Simon vents his virtuous rage in a page, which he thus concludes:—"Seeing so many depredations and no vacancy to be hoped for, I asked the Duke of Orleans to add 12,000 livres to the appointments of my government of Senlis, which was only worth 1,000 crowns, and I obtained it at once."

Luxury

Of what use are riches if not for enjoyment and show? The abundance of securities, some real, others fictitious, but having all the power of money, developed an unbridled luxury. There was a time when the Parisians seemed to be the actors in an immense fairy scene. As if by incessantly renewed changes of scene, people with little or nothing were suddenly seen provided with magnificent palaces, titled estates, important offices, with the ordinary accompaniments of great wealth, lackeys and parasites, horses and mistresses. New houses sprang up out of the earth, old ones became young again as if by enchantment. Inside them the furniture was splendid. Gold and silver, fashioned by the labour of the best *artistes*, were scattered about in dazzling style. To form a correct idea of it, the royal declaration of the 18th February, 1720, should be read, which, to put an end to the useless consumption of precious materials, forbids jewellers to make, sell, or expose "any banisters, chair-legs, cabinets, tables, desks, stands, mirrors, pans, and irons, gridirons, fire-irons, branch chandeliers to light-stands, girandoles, brackets, chimney backs, perfumery pans, hand baskets, baskets, orange-tree boxes, flower pots, urns, vases, pincushions, boxes, pails, wash-hand basins, tumblers, soup tureens, pie dishes, stewpans, flasks or bottles; above all, to place on table oil flasks, dessert services, and all other articles of a similar kind, *in silver*, or plated with silver." Entering a room furnished in such a manner, should we not think ourselves transported to Mexico under the reign of Montezuma?

Besides the public vehicles, which were increased by 1,200, there were in the streets, especially in those about the Rue Quincampoix, an excessive number of splendid carriages. It is true that often enough these carriages were filled with those who had formerly mounted behind. Many anecdotes on this subject amused the public. The mother of the Regent speaks of a rich ex-footman who used occasionally to mount behind his own carriage by way of amusement. Law's coachman one day brought two respectable young men to his master, saying:—"I am going to leave you, Sir: you will want a coachman in my place. Here are two whom I know, and can recommend to you. Choose one, and I will take the other for myself." These new masters who were good judges of liveries, prided themselves on doing things in great style. We may judge of this by the edict of the 25th of December, which forbade servants, *under pain of chains and imprisonment*, to wear lace too broad, or silk or velvet waistcoats, or buttons of massive silver.

As for extravagance in dress, we must let Duhautchamp speak. "The Rue St. Honoré," says he, "which heretofore would have furnished wherewith to clothe all France and its neighbours, was then considered used up. No more velvet or gold stuffs were seen there. The commencement of winter had carried all that was to be found there into the shops. This season, otherwise so dull, possessed more brilliancy, in the days of the *Scheme*, than the finest spring, whether from the velvet dresses of all colours, lined with gold and silver tissues, or from the magnificent laces and embroidery: as for the jewels, their brilliancy dazzled all eyes at Court and at the theatres." The use of diamonds, precious stones, and pearls, became at last so immoderate, that it was thought proper to forbid their use except by special permission, under pain of confiscation of them, and 10,000 livres fine.

Fêtes, spectacles, and pleasures of all kinds multiplied in a manner calculated to intoxicate this frivolous society. "Would people believe," says Duhautchamp, "that there were stockjobbers who played as easily at piquet with 10,000 livres notes as if they were playing for 10 sous pieces?" A music-mad Mississippian named Denis Léroche married an actress and kept open house to the opera-singers of both sexes. The contractor Fargés, marrying a second time, together with his two daughters and his niece, celebrated the four weddings by a princely *fête*, of which his Chateau de Montfermeil was the scene. During eight days the rarest meats and the most exquisite wines were served in extraordinary profusion: choirs composed of the most skilful musicians, orchestras inviting to the dance, succeeded each other without cessation; and at night-time the apartments, gardens, and park, were illuminated by an enormous number of torches of white wax.

A Mississippian, who, without being the richest, surpassed all others by the charm of his good taste and elegant manners, was formerly a landscape painter. Duhautchamp, who knew him, speaks of him without giving his name, as if from a sort of respect: "He carried his magnificence so far, that most of the deeds related of him appear fabulous. His hotel in Paris, his gardens, his furniture, his equipages, the number of his servants of all degrees and professions, equalled those of the greatest princes. A certain jeweller declares that he supplied him with more than three millions worth of precious stones, without reckoning the beautiful diamond of the Count de Nocé for which he paid 500,000 livres, and a girdle buckle which a Jew sold him for the same sum. With regard to his furniture, being a connoisseur and of good taste, ho had selected the whole so well, that, to form an idea of the magnificence of his apartments, we must have recourse to descriptions which are used of fairy palaces. Not content with 4,000 marcs of silver and silver gilt service which he had first ordered, he found means to carry off from the jewellers that which had been made for the King of Portugal, under pretext that the agents of that prince had been wanting in punctuality of payment. Besides this magnificent table service, he furnished himself with stands, mirrors, braziers, orange-tree cases, flower pots, etc. Lastly, all his cooking utensils were of silver—not excepting the chamber pots. As for his upholstery, he took everything which could be imagined of that kind that was most precious. He had no less than eighty horses in his stables—his equipages equalled in number those of the grand Sultan.

The number of his servants was nearly ninety, amongst whom were comprised intendant, secretaries, steward, surgeon, *valets de chambre*, upholsterers, four young ladies as chamber maids, and for his grooms four footmen of birth very superior to that of their master. Even when he went to dine away from home, he had his own table served as sumptuously as if he were present. It was served with everything most exquisite, principally during the year 1720. He was supplied with young peas which had cost one hundred pistoles the pint. Nothing was wanting that the most voluptuous *gourmet* could think of. The desserts that were served were fitted to surprise the most expert mechanicians. Large fruits, which would have deceived the eyes of the most clear-sighted, were so artistically contrived that when any one, surprised at seeing a beautiful melon in winter, attempted to touch it, he caused a number of little fountains to spring up of different sorts of spirituous liquors which delighted the sense of smell, whilst the master of the house, pressing his foot on a concealed spring, made an artificial figure walk round the table and pour out nectar to the ladies, before whom he was made to stop. In a word," says Duhautchamp, in conclusion, "I doubt whether the famous feasts of Antony and Augustus, so vaunted in history, had anything more rare than those which our fortunate millionaire took a pleasure in giving."

Feastings

Easy gains had made the habit of feasting general. People ate more; and every one in his station made greater pretensions to taste in selecting his food. The Parisians were very little disposed to self-mortification when the Lent of 1720 arrived. Never had the consumption of meat been more considerable; it was scarce at the butchers' shops when the price rose from ten to fourteen sous the pound. "The number of those who ate meat without any necessity, and through scandalous abuse," says Buvat, under the date of 27th of March, "was so excessive, that in eight days more than 800 oxen were consumed, without reckoning four times as many sheep, without reckoning calves, fowls and game, just as if they had been in the midst of the carnival." At the houses of some upstarts, quite Homeric- feasts were made. Madame Chaumont entertained so many people at her Château D'Ivry, that they consumed every day an ox, two calves, six sheep, and other things in proportion.

At the instance of the clergy, an order was given to the police to redouble the surveillance that they exercised over the dealers in provisions during the days of abstinence. These folks, being unable to carry on their trade at their own houses, had an understanding with the servants of great mansions, which were not exposed to domiciliary visits. They cooked the forbidden meats in the kitchens of private dwellings, and had them carried about town by servants in livery, or by the soldiers on guard at the houses of the great nobles. The contrivance having been discovered, severe measures were taken to repress it. By an order of the Lieutenant of Police, dated the end of February, 1720, "cooks were forbidden to take refuse in any royal or privileged house, nor in any hotel, there to prepare, sell or distribute any sort of meat under pain of six months' imprisonment, forfeiture of their freedom of the city, and 3,000 livres fine, payable jointly by them and by the cooks or others who had given them refuge in the said hotels or royal houses; and the penalty of the galleys was pronounced with respect to soldiers surprised with meat which they were fraudulently carrying about." The greed of gain nevertheless escaped the vigilance of power.

Marriages

One of the most surprising effects of the Scheme was to open to upstarts, scarcely yet "polished up," the ranks of the highest nobility. The Duke de la Vrilliere, Secretary of State, and member of the Council of the Regency, bestowed Madlle de Sainte-Hermine, his relation, on a native of Lyons, named Panier, who changed his name on purchasing an estate. One of the inventions of the age was a *redeemable marriage* (marriage à réméré), an amusing example of which is related in the following terms in the MS. Journal of the advocate Marais:—"The Marquis d'Oise, of the house of Villars-Brancas, entered into a proposal of marriage with a little girl two years old, daughter of André the Mississippian. The betrothal was made with the consent of the two families. The Marquis was to have an annuity of 20,000 livres until the marriage took place, and even in case it never took place. If it took place, the dowry was to be four millions. Little girls would no longer have dolls, but asked for Marquises of Oise to play with." The Marquis enjoyed the annuity; and, doubtless, found in André's subsequent decline an excuse for not completing the marriage, which never took place.

Public opinion manifested itself with severity against one of the members of the house of de Bouillon, the Count d'Evreux, engaged in an affair of this kind. This nobleman, in pressing need of money, had married the daughter of the elder Crozat, twelve years of age. After the nuptial ceremony, the young bride had been taken back to the convent, and the husband had received two millions, with more to come thereafter. Then sprung up the *Scheme*, thanks to which the Count d'Evreux gained five millions. He hastened to restore to the father the earnest money he had received, and sought to procure a nullification of the marriage, on account of misalliance. Crozat, it is true, had been a footman; but he was a man of incontestable merit, honourably enriched, very generous, and one of the two or three citizens who had offered some millions in the midst of the embarrassments which followed the death of Louis XIV. His daughter in the convent had become an accomplished lady. The father and daughter were both congratulated on having escaped the alliance of the Count d'Evreux.

Female Applicants

In the eyes of the wonder-stricken multitude, the author of so many prodigies was for some time a wizard, a superhuman being, a demi-god, in whose honour they professed a kind of worship. The Academy of Sciences chose him for one of its members. As he passed along, people cried out, "God save the King and Monseigneur Law."

He was overwhelmed with suppliant flattery in prose and verse; even his footmen were flattered. People wore his livery to be introduced at the Bank, and get credit in the Rue Quincampoix. "Law's antechamber," says the historian Duhautchamp, "was never empty of noblemen and ladies, whose sole occupation seemed to be a desire to pay court to him. Nothing appeared incredible any longer; and who ever has not been an eye-witness of it, seems to have a right to regard the whole as a dream. *Apropos* of this, I recollect that Miss Law (who was yet only five or six years old) determined to give a ball. Every one of the highest distinction went there, and people were rather surprised to see the Pope's Nuncio arrive among the first, make his obeisance and congratulate the little queen of the ball with a gracious kiss. Women, sad to relate, especially distinguished themselves in this concourse of adulation and baseness. Duclos declares that he has seen women of rank seated on the box of the carriage of the lady whom the Scotchman had presented as his wife, though he was not married. Many anecdotes of the same kind are related in the letters of the dowager Duchess of Orleans. "Law," she says, "is so pursued that he has no rest night or day. A Duchess has kissed his hand before everybody. And if Duchesses act thus, how will other women kiss him?"

Some anecdotes, related by the same Princess, will give an idea of the tricks that were invented to get at this dispenser of riches. A lady, not having been able to get an invitation to Madame de Simiane's, where Law was to dine, passed before the house in her carriage, and made her coachman and footmen shout 'Fire.' Instantly everybody left the hotel to learn where the fire was. Law ran out also. Directly the lady saw him she sprang from her carriage to speak to him. But Law, who saw through the trick, adroitly disappeared.

Another lady, driving to Law's residence in a carriage with the intention of being upset there, cried out to her coachman:—"Upset I say, upset, you rascal!" Law having run out to assist her, she confessed that she had acted thus to procure an interview with him. Like king Midas, whom the gift of changing everything to gold exposed to the chance of dying of hunger, the financier could not find time to exist. Harassed in the *salons* whenever he showed himself, pursued in the streets, tracked into his apartments by women who introduced themselves there by force or contrivance, and who waited there night and day till they met their victim, poor Law saw Countesses and Marchionesses suddenly rising round him at the very times when solitude was most needful to him. The Regent's mother relates things on this subject, which she could entrust confidentially to her friends in Germany, but which cannot be written in a French book.

The greatest proof of the admiration inspired by Law, and of the influence which he exercised over his contemporaries, is shown by the attempts made on every side to imitate him. Other nations voluntarily inoculated themselves with the disease which had attacked France. In Germany, Holland, and above all, England, people were found who discovered the secret of enriching private persons while freeing the State from its debts, and everywhere this mystification was made a pretext for a wild speculation. But it would be unjust not to point out an essential difference between Law and his foreign imitators.

In England, for example, the speculation had no other character than that of a fierce and blind cupidity.[5] Law,

---

5. London had its Rue Quincampoix in 1720: it was a long street called Exchange Alley. As soon as any stock had been openly quoted on this open-air Exchange, brokers went hawking it from door to door, not only

and some friends about him who formed his school, had as much generosity as good faith. Financial innovations had never been anything in their eyes but a means of arriving at political improvements. Law had a presentiment of reforms to be accomplished, and a sympathy for the multitude, and these raise him, at all events by intelligence and good intentions, far

---

in the towns but in the country, so that the rage for speculation was communicated to the whole population. Anderson, the historian of English commerce, speaks in these terms of this contagions frenzy:—"Persons of quality of both sexes were passionately engaged in these trickeries; noblemen had appointments with their agents and sharebrokers at coffeehouses and taverns: ladies went with the same object to their drapers and milliners. The first comer might hire a room, or a coffee-house parlour in the neighbourhood of the alley, and open a subscription-book for anything relating more or less to commerce, manufactures, plantations, or some supposed invention; and if he took care to advertise them the night before in the newspapers, he had a chance of disposing of many millions of his imaginary shares in a few hours. The confusion was so great in the crowd of Exchange Alley, that often the same share varied ten percent at one end of the street and the other."

The principal support of the stockjobbing was the shares of the South Sea Company, which, independently of its commerce, speculated in the redemption of a part of the State's debts. Its capital was raised to 950 millions of francs, (38 millions sterling), an enormous sum, which charlatanism increased tenfold since certain shares of £100 sterling rose to £1,000. The high price of these shares rendering them unattainable by slender purses, a host of secondary operations were contrived. The single year, 1720, saw more than 200 companies hatched in London, half of which went so far as to get into credit and issue their paper. Some enterprises went beyond all bounds. For example, a company of insurance against fire, to popularise its shares, issued them at the low rate of two shillings and sixpence. They rose to £8 sterling.

above the Statesmen of his time.

Law as a Reformer

"The ruling idea of Law," says the Count de la Mark, "was to suppress the cost and importunities of extortion, which hindered the communication of one province with another, and to substitute in its place a liberty which should encourage trade while assisting the people."

He therefore undertook to establish unity and equality of taxation, substituting for the various and arbitrary imposts, a single royal tax (*denier royal*) proportioned to each man's means. This plan, suggested by the "royal tithe" of Vauban, was first put into practice in the Election de Saintes, when two hundred and seventy parishes were scheduled by the comptroller of la Rochelle. Means were found to impede the experiment. Law, at least, equalised the public charges as much as possible, by making the Indian Company reimburse the sums received for exemption from taxation; after this he was enabled to revoke by an order of the 19th of February, all existing immune ties. Remission was, at the same time, made to needy taxpayers of eighty millions of taxes in arrear.

The minister Pontchartrain said to Louis XIV: "When it pleases your Majesty to create an office, God creates a fool to purchase it." In virtue of this maxim they coined money for thirty years, by selling to the first bidder the right of intervention in private transactions. The offices connected with trade were perhaps as numerous in Paris as the people engaged in it. There were hundreds of sworn cloth-measurers, controllers of all sorts of tallow, examiners of all sorts of oil, sworn trussers of hay, measurers of coal, commissaries for the piling of wood, examiners, markers and measurers of wood, carved or for building, markers of paper, inspectors of bridges and channels, sworn gilders, sworn criers of burials, verifiers of salt pork examiners of pigs' tongues, inspectors for beef, veal, mutton, poultry, fish—each having his special office. There was above all, in the trade in drinks, an immense phalanx of examiners, gaugers, tasters, dischargers, rollers of barrels, clearers, etc., with controllers to inspect those who tasted, gauged, discharged, rolled and cleared. In fact, all these officers were nothing less than annuitants, who interfered by authority in sales and purchases, so as to recover the interest of the sums they had advanced to government.

From the month of September, 1719, to the month of April, 1720, Law dictated a series of decrees tending to the abolition, with indemnity, of all these vexatious taxes. For example, the suppression of the charges and offices created on the ports, quays, and markets of Paris had the effect of immediately lowering, by 30 to 40 percent, the price of wood, coal, hay, grain, corn, meat, game, poultry, fish, eggs, butter, salt, and cheese.

Various combinations, to which the Indian Company generously lent itself, brought about the reduction of the duties on leather, oil, and tallow. Different taxes on navigation and transports were equally abolished. A decree, abolishing duties on grain, vegetables, and eatables of all kinds transported from one province to another, was an approach to the abolition of inland custom houses.

The import duty on sea-coal coming from England was reduced for the advantage of manufactures. All duties on wines, in Paris, were converted into a single tax on the import, at the rate of twenty-three livres the muid of wine arriving by water, and twenty livres by land carriage. It is about one-third of what is now paid.

The Indian Company, in the firm conviction of its promoter, was to be the instrument of general prosperity. A decree of the 29th of December, freed the hemp trade and exempted it from all duties, octrois, tolls, and at the same time authorised the Company to open, in the principal provincial towns, warehouses where hemp of good quality should be received and paid for, in whatever quantities it might be offered, at the rate of thirty to thirty-five livres the cwt. The object was to provide, on the one hand, a certain outlet to agriculture, and on the other an inexhaustible supply for spinning and weaving, which at this period were the occupations of poor people. Although it had acquired the monopoly of the sale of tobacco, the Company contenting itself with the custom's dues, allowed it to be manufactured and traded in by wholesale or retail. It equally gave up its privilege of selling beaver furs, and obtained a decree suppressing the existing duties on silks, both of home and foreign growth.

The persecutions and distress of the preceding years had forced many Frenchmen to expatriate themselves: their return was now facilitated by requesting Captains of ships to take charge of them for six livres a day, payable by the treasurers of the Navy.

Advances were made at the rate of 2 percent to manufacturers and traders honourably known. Two millions were devoted to the release of prisoners for debt. Restitution was made of the sums seized by the Chamber of Justice to those merchants who were in a condition to prove that they had taken no part in the alleged wrongs.

So much liberality on the part of the government, coinciding with the development of luxury among private persons, communicated an almost inordinate activity to industry. The number and importance of the manufactures increased by one-half. The first phase of this movement was very brilliant. Every one was astonished to find himself able to pay his debts. The number of failures diminished by three-fourths in 1719: there were 1,600 real distresses levied in all Paris.

The public works took an unusual and very intelligent flight: the bridge of Blois was constructed: the canal of Burgundy was dug: barracks were built, for the first time, to relieve citizens from having to lodge soldiers in their houses. It even appears that the idea of transforming Paris into a seaport dates back to Law, to judge, at least, from this note by Buvat. "They are working at a canal at Elboeuf, by means of which they expect to make the tide of the sea flow up the Seine to within a short distance of Paris, so as to render the river more navigable from that side, and to carry goods on it at all times in abundance and less dear."

The Council was also occupied in restoring neglected lands to cultivation, by constraining mortmain proprietors, that is, ecclesiastical communities, to sell the immoveable property which they had acquired during the last hundred and twenty years.

According to Vauban:—"A tenth of the population was reduced to mendicity, and begged most effectually." Thanks to the *Scheme*, it was considered probable that there might be an end to pauperism. We read, in a plan for the organisation of the general police of the kingdom, that sturdy mendicants should be made useful in the colonies; and, for the remainder, it was proposed "to establish hospitals at every six leagues, where these poor people should be received, fed, and taken care of by the inhabitants of the district, they being obliged to contribute according to each one's means."

A real benefit dates again from this time, and proceeds, perhaps, from the same inspiration: it is the establishment of gratuitous instruction in the University of Paris, by means of the twenty-eighth part of the postal revenue, which was set aside for the payment of the professors. The Parisian population was so touched by this liberality: they so well understood its tendency, that they determined to celebrate it by a grand procession, in which all classes were represented, down to the humblest artisans.

These generous efforts, coinciding with the first successes of the *Scheme*, explain the dazzled state of the nation, and justify its temporary enthusiasm for the strange and powerful man who had produced such phenomena.

CHAPTER VI

DISENCHANTMENT

CHAPTER VI

DISENCHANTMENT

Opposition—Realisers

The golden age of the *Scheme* lasted about eight months, from June, 1719, to February, 1720. During this period, there was, in the greater part of the country, a glow of wellbeing, and a confidence in the future which contrasted triumphantly with the misery of the preceding years. At the same time the illusion was not general, nor the intoxication without its aftertaste. In such an upset, bruises were inevitable. The duped speculators, (and they were numerous), the annuitants, puzzled about the price of their compensations and falling into snares, a legion of clerks, registrars, fiscal employees, and justice-folks no longer of use, the old finance humiliated and threatened, Parliaments injured in their power and dignity, furnished elements for a formidable opposition.

The blows which first began to damage the *Scheme*, were aimed by those who owed their fortunes to it.

A victim to the infatuation it had called forth, the Company was bending under a burden beyond its strength. The capital of the shares at the fabulous prices they had attained in December, 1719, represented eleven to twelve billions; the annual amount to be paid, in order to furnish interest at 3 percent only on this sum, would have been 350 millions. The probable returns, admitting the success of all their operations, would scarcely have given 1 percent. The Banknotes did not represent, as they should in a nominal condition, securities at short dates, deposited in one's pocketbook to be converted immediately into cash; the issues were made without control with limits unknown to the public. Unless afflicted with the prevailing madness, it was easy to foresee a financial crisis. Every clear-sighted man perceived that the moment had arrived to put by his gains, by exchanging ideal riches for more substantial property. Then commenced the retreat of those who had been called *realisers*.

In the course of December, a manoeuvre, planned by foreign speculators, kept up the shares for a fortnight at between 18,000 and 20,000 livres. They profited by this to sell: their example was followed by the most opulent of the French Mississippians. All these stockjobbers throwing their shares at once into the market of the Rue Quincampoix, collected immense sums in Banknotes, and immediately rushed to the Bank to exchange their notes for silver.

Surprised at this conduct, which he might nevertheless have expected, Law set himself to work to counteract it. By acts which followed closely on one another from the 1st of October, he gave all sorts of advantages to the possession of paper, and rendered as disagreeable as possible the use of coined money. It would be as tedious as useless to enumerate all the measures of this kind. It is sufficient to say, that, in a few months, thirty-three edicts, decrees, and declarations were published to fix the price of gold and silver, regulate the use of jewellery and plate, and arbitrarily control the circulation.

Law Becomes a Minister

The danger became daily more imminent; Law resolved to take power into his own hands, so as to defend himself with more vigour and precision. Protestants not being admitted to exercise public functions in France, the Scotchman was converted to Catholicism, (on the 5th of January, 1720), and got himself nominated Controller-General of Finance. Thenceforth, he was seen, as it may be said, fighting personally against his enemies. He went to the Rue Quincampoix with a train of noblemen, partisans of the *Scheme*; he raised the spirits of the dealers, from whom he received an ovation; he put himself into direct communication with the public, through little pamphlets of great ability; he multiplied administrative expedients to induce annuitants and officers subjected to the reimbursements, to throw their capital into the *Scheme*, so as to replace the great capitalists.

The efforts of the minister, betraying his embarrassments and his fears to the eyes of the experienced, served only to increase the distrust. The depreciation of specie could no longer stop the realisers. What did it signify to one who sold his share at the rate of 20,000 livres, to receive only 15,000 in intrinsic value, when this share had only originally cost him a few hundred livres? Moreover, the trouble taken to keep the shares up at a high price only profited the great capitalists by giving them time to dispose of their shares to advantage. The Bank, in the hope of propping up its tottering credit, having affected a redoubled promptitude in the payment of its notes, the sellers had all sorts of facilities for getting hold of gold and silver.

Forestalments

A certain number of speculators found themselves suddenly overwhelmed with treasure. Each one hastened to place it in safety. The foreigners retreated, carrying away millions. The Frenchmen at first resorted to immoveable property. Whatever was for sale in houses, hotels, rural property, and territorial estates, was bought up directly. New men, mostly sprung up from a very low origin, had so much gold to offer, that many of the nobility determined to sell their family estates. These investments being made at the rate of 1 to 2 percent, the price of landed property was soon quintupled; many landlords, crippled with debt and threatened with foreclosures, had only to dispose of a small portion of their lands to be free. The author of the *Scheme*, himself yeilding to this movement, made some important acquisitions. Several millions were laid out by him in the purchase of the lordships of Ligny, Boissy, Domfront, Tancarville, Lamarche, Guermande, and eight other estates. A less firmly convinced man would have made investments in foreign countries. In the situation of Law, to purchase landed property was to show the confidence he had in the system, and offer, in some measure, guarantees to the public.

For want of lands and houses for sale, the realisers sought out objects of value with avidity. It is this which explains the scandalous and ridiculous extravagance of this period. With many people, extravagance was a speculation. The annuities attached to public offices furnished others with a means of investment. After they had used up all that the dealers could offer them in jewels, plate, furniture, upholstery, horses, carriages, and works of art, they began to buy up common merchandise, stuffs, groceries, and even books. A stockjobber, named Lagrange, bought an entire edition of *Bayle's Dictionary*.

The forestallers paying as much as possible in notes, trade was soon inundated with paper, which, instead of the additional value which decrees gave it, underwent a gradual depreciation. They even began to quote goods at different prices, according as the payment should be in notes or specie; and as, in such circumstances, retail trade is regulated by the highest prices, the most necessary provisions of life became unattainable by poor people. In January, 1720, common bread was sold at four sous the pound. The dearness of meat caused so marked a discontent among the public, that Law at one time entertained the idea of entering into competition with the butchers to compel them to lower their prices.

Wood and coal were so much dearer, as the carmen charged as much for carrying them as the dealer for selling them. Candles, fixed at eight sous six deniers the pound, were sold at twenty sous, though tallow had been imported from England in large quantities. The decrees that were made to fix the prices of many things were of no avail: for instance, hackney-coachmen, whose charge was fixed at thirty sous the hour, asked double that sum.

The Mississippians, accustomed to squander gold, did not even notice these little details. But it was not the less a matter of the last importance to the multitude of those who had not dabbled in stockjobbing. To this state of uneasiness, from which the people began to suffer, was added a more direct cause of irritation. To explain its origin, we must return to the most prosperous days of the system.

The Emigrants

On the 19th of September, 1719, the bells ringing in full peal, and resounding with their merriest changes, told the inhabitants of the Quartier St. Martin that there was a fête in their parish. In an instant everybody was at the doors and windows—"What's it about? A marriage? Then it must be a princess?—No: this morning a hundred and eighty young girls have been taken from the prison of St. Martin des Champs; all the young rogues from the prisons of Paris have been led out in front of them. Each has made her choice, and you are entreated, good Parisians, to assist at the nuptial benediction which is about to take place."

Judge of the curiosity awakened by such news, and of the crowd, which in a few moments blocked up the church and the neighbouring streets! The excitement of the situation, the fears and hopes of the wedded couples in this conjugal lottery, no doubt enlivened the ceremony. But, alas, on coming out of the church, the inflexible police were in attendance with pretty little chains which they had gallantly forged for the occasion. These unfortunate young folks, still decked with flowers, were chained together two and two, husband and wife; they were formed in rank under the escort of twenty archers, who conducted them through the most populous streets to the extremity of the Faubourg St. Marceau.

The chains were a little too much, and threw a cloud over the picture. They were suppressed in the expeditions which followed. On the 18th of September, two hundred more of these extemporised couples were sent off. The women, to whom the candid Buvat is very indulgent in calling them "young ladies of little virtue," had their heads dressed *à la Fontange*, with ribbons of jonquille colour: they stood upright with their hands on their hips in wagons, round which walked the young men decked with their ladies' colours—that is, each with a jonquille ribbon at his button-hole, and a jonquille cockade in his hat. "The young ladies, while traversing Paris, sang like creatures without care, and called by their names those whom they fancied they recognised as old acquaintances, without even sparing their collars." It is easy to imagine the eagerness of the Parisian population to see such a procession, the coarse refrains caught up in chorus, the bursts of laughter at each sally, and at each person recognised. But, again, what lessons for the crowd! What muddy traces left in minds open to every impression!

This theatrical show was what we should nowadays call

an advertisement for the benefit of the *Scheme*. Amongst the number of privileges possessed by it, the Indian Company reckoned in the first rank that of sending every year to the Mississippi 9,000 persons, of whom 6,000 were Europeans, mostly French, and 3,000 negroes. As Saint-Simon says: "By turning and hoisting this Mississippi about in all ways, not to say by playing all sorts of juggleries under its name, they wished, after the example of the English, to make effectual establishments in these vast countries. It was to people them that they carried off from Paris and all parts of the kingdom, vagrants, sturdy beggars, men and women, and a number of public prostitutes. If all this had been done with wisdom and discernment, it would have accomplished the object proposed, and rid Paris and the provinces of a useless and dangerous burden; but they set to work with such violence and rascality, that it excited a great deal of murmuring. They had not taken the least care to provide subsistence for so many unfortunate wretches on their way, nor even in the places destined for their embarkation: they shut them up in barns at night, without giving them anything to eat, and in ditches, wherever they might happen to be, and from whence they could not get out. They uttered cries which excited pity and indignation; but the gifts of charity being insufficient for them, and still more what their conductors gave them, a frightful number of them died on all sides."

According to the reports current among the public, the sufferings of the journey could only have been half the evil. It is related that a portion of these emigrants, thrown into bad ships, were shipwrecked on the passage, and that 1,500 French of both sexes landed at the Mississippi were slaughtered by the natives.

Such rumours penetrating even into the prisons excited there a natural feeling of exasperation. There was a riot in more than one of them. On the 2nd of January, 1720, thirty-eight prisoners of both sexes, or rather nineteen married couples, placed in the gaol of St. Martin des Champs, while waiting for their departure, "seized the gaoler, his keys, and all the rest of his property, and set themselves at liberty, to escape from the pilgrimage to Mississippi."[1] One hundred and fifty girls had been conducted to Rochelle with great trouble. At the signal for embarkation a redoubled fury seized them; they sprung furiously on their conductors and attacked them with feet and hands, nails and teeth. "The archers were obliged to fire on these poor creatures, six of whom were killed and twelve wounded, which intimidated the others so much that they submitted to embark."[2]

Still sadder scenes perhaps took place in the South of France. The governors of Provence, Dauphiny, Languedoc, and Gascogny, had orders to carry off girls of suspected character, and send them to Marseilles. The number of these unfortunates who found themselves together there, was, alas, very great! But it was allowed that it was impossible to introduce into a rising colony elements so corrupted. They conveyed these desolate and helpless women great distances away from their own country, and they became whatever they could.

The vagabonds and rogues, already arrived at Mississippi, having caused nothing but disorder, the Company changed its method of recruiting, and instead of people of vicious lives they condemned to exile those whose only crime was poverty. The houses of refuge for the poor and mendicants were very numerous at this period. In Paris alone, Bicêtre, la Pitié, la Salpêtrière, les Enfans Trouvés, and above all the great depôt of mendicity established in 1656, under the name of the General Hospital, might, it was said, supply 4,000 emigrants. The

---

1. Buvat

2. Buvat

religious congregations, who governed these establishments, made use of the labour of their pensioners; there was some resistance to be feared on their part. Skilful in managing conflicting interests, Law went and visited the hospitals in great state, and removed all difficulties by an offer of three millions. Other measures were taken to increase the number of recruits. Woe to him who could not show his means of existence. A decree ordered footmen and people in service out of place, to furnish themselves with a certificate from their late masters, stating the date of their dismissal, and (incredible as it seems) if they were out of employment for four days they were considered as vagrants, and liable to be sent off to the colonies.

Orders were transmitted at the same time to the juries of the Companies of artisans, to watch that each master renewed every eight days the certificate that he had to give to his assistants and apprentices, in default of which the latter being taken by the archers would be sent to the Mississippi. Lastly, Controllers of Provinces were ordered to cause a list to be prepared by the clergy of all the vagabonds, idle fellows, and libertines who were to be found in each parish, under penalty of a fine of 500 livres against each clergyman who failed to furnish the exact particulars.

These measures spread a vague anxiety, especially among the poorer classes. Instead of the wild merriment which the first expeditions had encouraged, they felt now a sinking of the heart on seeing those herds of human beings pass by, who were being sent across the seas. One day it was a long procession of a hundred orphan girls, fourteen or fifteen years of age, poor children who, perhaps, had happy dreams because they had been promised "a bed furnished with four sheets, and several household utensils." More often things happened thus, as Buvat relates, under the date of the 27th of February, 1720:—"Departure of six hundred young people of both sexes taken from the Hospitals of Paris.

The young men on foot, chained two and two, and the girls in wagons. This troop was followed by eight carriages filled with well-dressed young people, some of whom wore gold and silver lace; and the whole were escorted by thirty archers well armed." While pitying these unfortunates, each man began to think of himself. Who was sure not to share their lot?

The Bandoliers of the Mississippi

To seize those alleged vagabonds, whom authority delivered up to them body and soul, the Company had been authorised to set on foot a regiment of archers to whom they gave, besides their equipment, twenty sous a day wages, and one pistole for every person arrested. It is known how troops were recruited at this period. Some old soldier, calling himself captain, beat up the quays and streets, explored the taverns and bad houses, and made a few pieces of gold and silver dazzle the eyes of the rogues whom he met, and enrolled them after some drink. In this manner armies were obtained with plenty of energy, but very little morality.

The Indian Company was not very fortunate in its selections, as it appears. The archers whom it enrolled were a set of downright rascals, who, for a pistole, would have arrested a saint. Bravely dressed in a large blue coat, with three-cornered hat bound with silver stuck on one side, a sword suspended crossways from a large bandolier, like those of the Suisses of the church, armed with a bayonetted gun, and two pocket pistols—such were the men who were called in the streets, "The Bandoliers of the Mississippi." They scoured the pavements by files of a dozen, and woe to whoever fell in their hands. Poor people, who could not get any one to redeem them were apprehended, taken to prison, and there were ten livres a head gained. As for those good-natured citizens whom the report of it enraged, they found means to frighten them, and did not let them off without ransom. According to Saint-Simon's account, it was sufficient to slip a purse into an archer's hand, and whisper a word in his ear to get any enemy of whom you wished to be rid carried off. It was the slavery of the whites organised in the streets of Paris.

Disturbances

Public report exaggerating the evil, a sort of terror resulted which spread from Paris to the provinces. The rumour in the villages was, that they were going to take away two girls out of every three above ten years of age, and it is easy to conceive the excitement that such news caused. It was said in Paris that more than 5,000 persons had disappeared since the month of April, amongst others many who had never made a trade of begging, such as artisans, workmen, and even a hundred newly-arrived girls.[3]

There was, at that time, in the Quartier St. Denis, a pious house called the Hospital of St. Catherine, where good religious ladies received for three days, lodged and fed gratuitously, young girls from the country, who had come to Paris to enter into service. Most of the citizen families went to this house to choose what servants they needed, and the reciprocal engagement was made there to some extent under the seal of religion. The disappearance, real or supposed, of a hundred of these poor girls, had already set the Quartier in commotion, when it was heard that the archers were dragging away the son of a M. Capet, a rich grocer of the Rue St. Honoré, as well as a young and pretty girl, the daughter of a lieutenant of the watch. It then became impossible to restrain popular exasperation.

---

3. Buvat—under the date of the 10th of May, 1720. There was, no doubt, exaggeration in these popular rumours; but it is not uninteresting to listen to their echo at the distance of more than a century.

"The populace and the shopkeepers" (so our chroniclers express themselves) "making arms of everything, rushed with fury on the archers: twenty were killed on the spot: a much greater number dangerously wounded were carried dying into the Hôtel Dieu."

The impunity of this bloody outbreak was the sole concession made to public opinion. To calm the excitement of the multitude, the government had it proclaimed by sound of trumpet on the 4th of May, 1720, that, in future, each brigade of bandoliers would be accompanied by an officer of police marching at their head, and two archers of the provost serving as corporals. The Parliament, on its part, required that the list of persons imprisoned should be submitted to it each week, reserving to itself the right of setting at liberty those who were not rightfully condemned. Lastly, under pretence of surveillance, the lieutenant of police enjoined the syndics of the six corps of tradesmen to bring him, with the least possible delay, a list of names of the children, shop-boys, and apprentices of each trade—a precaution which was not much calculated to reassure the Parisian citizens. In spite of these appearances of guarantee, the seizures for the Mississippi continued to be carried on with as much rascality and inhumanity as in the past, to the great injury of Law and the Regent, whose names were mingled with the popular imprecations.

These violent deeds were so much the more to be condemned, because they had not even the excuse of utility. A new land is not to be cultivated by a set of rebellious persons habituated to disorderly lives. On the contrary, for such a purpose, willing people of sound and vigorous constitutions are required.

Nearly all the women forcibly Sent to the Mississippi soon died there of disease or despair. The men, more resolute, formed connections with the native women. Some of them found in their companions the most tender and ingenuous devotion. At the same time, it would not do to trust them too much, as is proved by a trage-comic episode which at one time attracted the notice of the Parisians.

The Daughter of the Sun, and Dubois the First

As a specimen of the effects of the *Scheme*, they had brought to Paris, from the shores of the Mississippi, ten male savages and one female. The latter was a Queen, the descendant of an illustrious family called *the Race of the Sun*. The men had great success. They caught on foot, in sight of the King and the Court, a stag which was started in the Bois de Boulogne. They several times performed the dances of their country at the Theatre-Italien.

Whilst the public were being amused with these frivolities, political men carried their views much further. They determined to marry the Queen of the Missouri to a Frenchman, so as to found an Empire tributary to France, and, perhaps, a rival to the English power in the New World. The Queen was young and of striking beauty. Only one drawback was known about her: it was that, by her rank as daughter of the Sun, she had the right of putting her husband to death directly he began to be troublesome to her. In spite of this clause many aspirants offered themselves, and the Queen chose, out of the number, a brave and handsome sergeant of the guards, named Dubois. A few days afterwards she abjured her errors in the Church of Notre-Dame, received baptism, and was married with great ceremony. But, alas, scarcely had Dubois I, King of the Missouri, arrived in his dominions, before the capricious daughter of the Sun had him put to death, and perhaps eaten. Thus fell one of the ornaments of the crown of the Mississippians.

Discredit of the Paper

Although the share was still at 10,000 livres, although the conversion of the notes was not suspended, the realisers appeared in such haste to empty their desks of them, that the alarm spread as a sort of contagion. From the month of March tradesmen began to ask, according to the degree of their alarm, 30, 50, or 100 percent, more when notes were presented to them in payment. In Lyons, Rouen, Bordeaux, and Lille, and many places of secondary importance, they refused to receive the paper, and the discontent went even to the extent of a disturbance. Fears were entertained for the supplies of provisions in the great towns. On the market of Poissy, the tradesmen wished one day to carry off the cattle: there was scarcely time to run to the keeper of the seals, who hastened to send bags of gold and silver so as to prevent the outbreak of alarm which a want of meat would have caused in Paris.

At the point to which things had now arrived, it would have needed a miracle to save the *Scheme*. Perhaps some manoeuvre might have been thought of to secure the assistance of the parvenus in supporting the Bank and the Company, either by offering them the bait of a fresh profit or frightening them with the consequences of a financial catastrophe. But, as if the despotism with which he was armed had obscured the usual clearness of his judgment, Law resolved to crush all resistance, and to impose faith in his paper by constraint—an enterprise as absurd as it was odious.

The Crown-Pieces are Proscribed

A decree of the 28th of January, directed against those who were monopolising the specie, ordered a debasement of the coinage (the small pieces excepted) to fifty-four livres to the marc of silver. At the same time the Indian Company was authorised to make domiciliary visits, so as to seize for its own benefit the old pieces which many people refused to submit to be recoined. In cases where the seizure was made on the information of a third party, the whole of the sum confiscated was to be handed over to the informer.

By a second decree of the 27th of February, it was ordered, "that no person, of whatever estate or condition, not even any religions or ecclesiastical community, should keep more than 500 livres in coined money or ingots, under pain of confiscation of the excess, and of a fine of 10,000 livres." The goldsmiths and jewellers themselves could not exceed these limits except by special permission. All persons were forbidden to make payments above 100 livres in anything but Banknotes. A few days afterwards, (the 5th of March), as if to leave less regret to those who were about to be separated from their crown-pieces, a general debasement of the coinage was ordered in the proportion of eighty livres to the marc of silver.

Lastly, a royal declaration, dated the 11th of March, abolished entirely the use of gold specie from the 1st of May following, and the use of silver specie, with the exception of the small pieces, from the 1st of August. The prohibition against keeping gold and silver in one's house was renewed with redoubled severity, and for the legal value of the money kept were prescribed a series of arbitrary variations, so multiplied that it would have required a great deal of calculation to know what the money in one's pocket would be worth in a fortnight, or in a month. It was evidently wished to render the use of metallic money as disagreeable as possible, so as to disgust the public with it. Law had reached that degree of aberration which foretells the approaching fall of Statesmen.

These vexatious measures brought a great deal of silver back; and as the Bank did not pay out more than 500 livres at a time, since this sum was the maximum that an individual could possess, the cash in hand was soon considerable. But this was to the benefit of the great people for whom laws at this period were not made. The Prince de Conti sent to the Bank three carts, which returned full of crown-pieces. The Duke de Bourbon drew out twenty-five millions. The Duke of Orleans having reproached them for this, and threatened them with confiscation, they replied haughtily that they awaited the people of justice. Visits were, indeed, made to their hotels, but nothing was seized, either because the specie had been well concealed, or the commissaries had been intimidated, or because there was nothing in this display of severity but a comedy played off before the eyes of the public.

Domiciliary Researches-Informers

As it was desired to frighten people of no consequence, so that they should bring in their silver of their own accord, these domiciliary researches were proceeded in with an affectation of rigour. One of the first victims was one of the directors of the Company, named Adine, at whose house they found 10,000 crowns. Besides this sum, which was confiscated, he paid the fine of 10,000 livres, and lost his employment. Woe to the Mississippians! Many of their former bankers, transforming themselves into informers, threw themselves on their track like hungry wolves. What a fine booty to denounce *a parvenu* at whose house they found, as at Sohier's, an old clerk of the papers, 6,000 marcs of gold and 20,000 marcs of silver—that is to say, more than six millions of francs of our money! A still larger sum was seized, 50,000 marcs of gold and silver, with four hundred beautiful gold watches, at the house of a shopkeeper, in the Rue Verrerie, named Dupin, whom they sent to prison with his wife. Examples of this kind, made noisily public, struck the imagination, and made timid people hasten to change their treasures for notes. The ex-chancellor, Pontchartrain, brought from his cellar 57,000 louis of ancient make, which were then worth seventy-two livres each, much to the amusement of the young courtiers, by whom he was not liked.

Precautions were also taken against furtive exportation. While searching some wagons which were on their way towards the frontiers of Switzerland, they seized forty millions in gold, which were carried to the Mint. The brothers Paris having obtained permission to send into Lorraine 600,000 livres to pay for some contract supplies, managed to pass seven millions to buy lands and estates there. "The keeper of the seals having had information of it, sent in haste after the conveyances, which were bought back and unloaded at the Bank. At the same time they went to the house of the brothers Paris, where they again found, it is said, a similar sum of seven millions, which were also confiscated for the benefit of the Indian Company." Such a capture from the sworn enemies of the *Scheme*, must have delighted the Scotchman; but the four sons of Aymon—it is thus the Paris were called—were people to take their revenge.

The great merchants, the bankers, the goldsmiths, and the many communities who obtained permission, through favour, to keep a larger sum in cash than 500 livres, were equally subject to visits; and, in case of contravention, lost the sum exceeding the amount authorised. The Notaries and Commissaries of the Chalêtet were exposed to a special surveillance; they carried away from their houses even the funds deposited with them by their clients. Many people had fancied that they had placed their money in safety by sending it, under pretence of pious works, to clergy, or into the convents. The contrivance was useless: the superiors of religious houses were addressed and admonished severely. "Many commissaries went and paid visits to the principal clergy of the city and suburbs of Paris, and there confiscated sums considerably above 500 livres, although these clergymen might say or represent that these moneys were the proceeds of charities which had been entrusted to them, to be distributed among the poor of their parishes: to which it was replied, with reason, that if they had distributed them as they ought, and might have done, the poor would have had assistance, and all this money would not have lain useless in their hands."

The louis and the crown-pieces voluntarily brought in, and in exchange for which the Bank gave notes, amounted to more than forty millions. As for the confiscations, we have no information as to their total produce. If we remark that the right of seizing everywhere sums exceeding 500 livres, and of enforcing also a fine of 10,000 livres, was carried out vigorously not only in Paris, but in all the provinces of the kingdom, it is very clear that the spoil must have been immense.

The Indian Company was only too well seconded by informers, although their reward was reduced to half the sum confiscated. The temptation was so much the stronger to base minds, because the traitor remained unknown, and could continue to shake the hand of the confiding friend whom he had robbed. Supposing they received notice of a concealment made in a cellar, the commissary began by turning over everything in the attics and the rooms, and it was only at the last moment, and as if by chance that he had the pickaxe applied to the place which had been pointed out to him. A wretched insupportable distrust congealed the ties of affection, as well as commercial transactions. The master felt himself at the mercy of his servant, the merchant of his clerk, the capitalist of his debtor. Informers inspired such a horror, that public opinion put them as it were out of the pale of the law. Many of them were assassinated without ordinary search being made to punish the perpetrators. The very author of the decree, the Regent, ordered a son to be thrown into prison who had informed against his own father. The President Lambert de Vermon, having one day solicited an audience with the Chief of the State, addressed him in a mysterious manner, saying, "My Lord, I am come to point out to you a man who has in his house 50,000 livres in gold." At these words the Prince drew back in surprise and disgust, "Ah! M. le President," he cried, "what a trade are you taking to!" "Prince," replied the old magistrate, "the energy of your expression proves to me that you share the sentiments of the nation on the law that you have made. For the rest, it is myself whom I denounce to you, and I hope that you will not refuse me the reward promised to informers." The President thus saved the half of his fortune.

An Orgie

The wealth and debauchery of some, the poverty and rage of others, the removal of the ordinary distinctions of classes, the commercial crisis, the seizures, the denunciations, and the confiscations, had profoundly disturbed society. Ill-regulated minds and public demoralization manifested themselves every day in extravagant or sinister deeds. A wild scene, the memory of which was aroused by one of the most melancholy events,[4] was considered by contemporaries as the prologue of a bloody drama, of which the following is the story. It is under this head that it should find a place here:—

"Monsieur Nigon, an advocate, who lodged in the cloister of St. Germain l'Auxerrois, having died on the 19th of October, 1719, and his bier being exposed, at seven o'clock in the morning, at the door of his lodging, covered with funeral cloths, and surrounded by tapers with candlesticks, and a holy water-pot of silver, they notified to the Duke d'Aremberg, a

---

4. This account is borrowed, often word for word, from the chronicles of the times, and especially Buvat, (vol. iii. of the folio copy, p. 1074.)—See also Duhautchamp.

young prince of the Pays-Bas, who lodged in a neighbouring house, that the priests of the parish were coming to take away the corpse of the deceased to bury it. The Duke, who had passed the night in drinking with four other noblemen, descended with them, followed by their footmen, each having a bottle of wine and a glass in his hand." They surrounded the coffin, and each one apostrophising the deceased—(a wretched parody of Don Juan)—"It is true, then, my dear Nigon, that you have let yourself die!—Dead, and of what? Of thirst, no doubt; what can any one die of but of thirst? To drink is to live! To drink is to come to life again! Leave that infernal black cloak and that black raven who is guarding you, and come with us." These proposals, and many others, which crossed one another, were accompanied by libations, which settled the chief of the band. The Duke d'Aremberg, luckily for him, tumbled down dead drunk. His companions took him by his four limbs; and, followed by the footmen, glasses and bottles in hand and napkins on arms, carried him in procession into his house.

Over-excited by these follies, and out of their senses, the madcaps returned to the charge, led by a young Count, a cousin of the Duke, and still followed by the footmen. The crowd, which began to collect, murmured, and tried to prevent such a scandalous proceeding. The Count cried out that he had a right to offer his friend Nigon something to drink since he had died of thirst. "He jumped upon the coffin, as on horseback, and having got hold of the holy water-pot, he poured the holy water on the dead man's head, crying out, 'here drink, drink, my poor Nigon.'" The others, under pretence of setting their friend at liberty, drew their swords; and, striking the coffin, upset the candlesticks, and tore away the drapery. "The priests, come to convey the body, were greatly astonished at beholding the deeds of these drunkards; and getting nothing but obscene remarks from them, set to work to carry the body in the best way they could. These noblemen and their people followed the convoy in the same equipage; and the corpse being placed in the church, they made the tour of it, and astonished the choir with allelujahs and requiems, alternately with chaunts."

The fact of another piece of extravagance was a diversion from this impiety. Several men of ripe age and serious aspect were crossing the square where the church stood, and approaching a house of respectable appearance. "Where are these rascals going?" cried the Count; "is there a Marionette theatre here?" They told him that the house in question is that of the Abbé Bignon, State Councillor, member of three academies, King's librarian, possessing himself a very valuable library, and that the most learned persons in France met at his house from time to time to discuss the most important questions. "Ah! the Abbé Bignon gives representations of Marionettes, does he? *Parbleu*! That's the thing for us." And off the mad fellows went, and made a row at the venerable Abbé's door, calling him by his name, wanting to get in to see the entertainment, and offering to pay for their places as became men of quality. The porter, says the chronicler, barricaded the door the best way he could, and put an end to the scandal by fetching the King's archers.

The clergy had lodged a complaint; but as soon as they recovered their proper senses, the rakes judged it prudent to go and humble themselves before the vicar, protesting that they had completely lost the use of their reason when they committed the crime, which they could not think of without horror. The vicar lent ear to this seeming repentance, and employed himself in getting the proceedings stopped. Buvat adds:—"The whole of this scene did not fail to be soon reported to the Duke of Orleans, to whom it afforded a capital subject for laughter, from the novelty of the thing, of which there had never before been an example."

But nobody cared to laugh in public, or at least among those numerous and obscure classes, where, in spite of the corruption instilled from all sides, were still to be found good people with simple honest souls. The adventure, soon spread about, caused among such people a feeling of sadness which was like the presentiment of some catastrophe. They said that such a profanation left unpunished by men would be chastised by God, and that evil would befall him who had committed it.

The Fair of St. Germain

It was observed, towards the end of the winter of 1720, that night attacks and daring assaults were more frequent than ordinarily. This evil growth was attributed to the sort of madness which seemed to seize the gamblers at the fair of St. Germain. The place of resort and of pleasure thus called consisted of several blocks of houses and shops of wood work, separated by passages which crossed one another at right angles, and opening at last into a square where the market of St. Germain has since been built. Being opened from the 3rd of February until Lent, this fair coincided with the rejoicings of the Carnival. The goods exhibited in the shops were but accessories; its principal attraction consisted in plays, curiosities, feasting places, cafés, and games of all sorts. Independently of certain taverns, which were really gambling-houses, they shuffled the cards and shook the dice-box in many of the shops; they played with money or goods; strangers invited one another to play; passers-by bet for or against the players; it was the fashion and the excitement of the place. In 1720 gambling was the rage, notwithstanding an order of the police threatened with a fine of 3,000 liyres those who should be caught playing at cards, dice, biribi, faro, lansquenet, and other games of chance. "The players," says Buvat, "thought nothing of staking on a card, or on the first throw of the dice, as much as 20, 30, 40, 50, and 60,000 livres, as if the notes with which their pocket-books were filled had no more value than bits of blank paper."

The Count De Horn

A young foreigner of distinction, living in the Rue Dauphine at the Hotel de Flandre, had played deeply, and with such ill-luck that superstitious people fancied he must have committed some crime. In the midst of his embarrassments, two of the companions of his debauches persuaded him to repair his losses by certain tricks at the expense of the other players who met in the Rue Quincampoix. Nothing was more easy than such an enterprise. The papers payable to bearer were negotiated without mediation, from hand to hand, between people who did not know one another, in a tavern or in a street. Numbers of persons carried considerable sums about them in shares for sale or Banknotes for payments.

For many days the three robbers, disguised as foreign merchants, mingled in the groups of stockjobbers to scent out their victims. Being addressed by a working upholsterer, named Lacroix, who acted as broker for anonymous speculators, they offered to deliver securities at a price which promised the poor fellow brilliant profits. A meeting was, therefore, fixed for the morrow at seven in the morning. On both sides there were reasons for being punctual. As they could not manage the affair in the open street, they exchanged offers of a bottle of wine at "the Wooden Sword;" this was the name of a tavern situate in a little alley which led from the Rue Quincampoix to the Rue St. Martin. The speculators having asked for a private room to make out their accounts, were conducted to one on the second floor, where breakfast was served. After the meal, the broker having taken out his pocketbook, crammed with 150,000 livres in Banknotes, one of the robbers left the room on some pretence, and remained on the staircase to keep watch. Another passing behind Lacroix's back, threw a napkin over his head, and hoisted it tightly to blind him and hold him. The third stabbed him ten times with his dagger.

A water carrier lodged on the third floor. Having heard suspicious noises, he hastened to inform the landlord of it. The latter, seeing the man who was keeping watch on the staircase take to flight on his arrival, turned the key of the door of the room where the crime had just been committed. Bold and active, the two assassins reached a beam which shored up the house, and glided down it into the street. The alarm had already been given. All the neighbourhood was in commotion. One of the fugitives, who had been wounded in getting down, and who was stained with blood, was arrested by the market people. The other, who had excited remarks by his wild air, thought to evade suspicion by going himself to the Commissary of Police, where he declared that he was a man of rank, and had been attacked by malefactors. The Commissary had respectfully taken down the deposition, and was preparing to show the noble stranger out, when the truth came to light. Denials soon became impossible. On one of the assassins the victim's pocketbook was found. At last the names of the guilty were known. The one who had escaped, and who was never taken, used to call himself the Chevalier de Lestang; he was the son of a Flemish banker. He who had struck the blows was a Piedmontese captain, named Laurent, Count de Mille. The name of the third was Antoine Joseph, Count de Horn, captain of cavalry, aged twenty-two years. He was descended from the famous Count de Horn, who shared with the Count d'Egmont the glory of the scaffold erected by the Duke of Alba: he was the second son of Emmanuel Philippe, Count and Prince de Horn and of Antoinette, Princess de Ligne. He was connected by family alliances with the Emperor of Germany, the Regent of France, and many sovereign houses, with the Châtillons, the Montmorencies, the Arembergs, with all the highest nobility in Europe.

For some days all other interest was absorbed in that of the frightful drama of the Rue de Venisse. In inquiring into the antecedents of the guilty men, it was discovered that the Count de Horn was that God-forsaken man who had taken the lead of his companions in debauchery, and committed the greatest scandals at the funeral of the advocate Nigon.

The nobility of Europe felt itself disgraced by the sentence which was about to break one of its members upon the wheel. We read in Buvat's Journal:—"The Post Office clerks declare that more than eight thousand letters have been received from Brussels, and other places of the Low Countries, addressed to princes, princesses, noble lords and ladies of the French Court, to solicit their intercession with the King and the Regent in favour of this unfortunate Count de Horn." By the time the letters arrived justice had already been done.

Earnest supplications were addressed to the Regent by the highest nobles of the Court. They exhausted judicial strategy to get a commutation of the sentence. The guilty man considered himself so much beyond the reach of justice, that he appeared before his judges with an almost indecent levity. Law, on the other hand, secretly insisted that an example should be made of him as a proceeding necessary, he said, to reassure the terrified speculators. The Regent opposed to all solicitations a firmness which did him credit. "When I have bad blood in me," said he to the relations who invoked the honour of their blood, "I have it drawn from me." It is to be believed, however, that, out of consideration for the family, he lent himself to a plan for saving the criminal, if not from deserved death, at least from the infamy of a public execution. Duclos says, on this subject:—When the relations or connections had lost all hope of altering the determination of the Regent, Prince de Robecq-Montmorency and Marshall d'Isenghien, with whom the condemned was most nearly connected, found means to penetrate into his prison, took poison to him, and exhorted him to avoid the disgrace of an execution; but he refused. "Go, then, miserable wretch," they said, leaving him, "you are only worthy to die by the hands of the executioner."

The Count and his accomplice were broken on the wheel on the Place de Grève, on Tuesday, the 26th of March, four days after the crime. Horn lived an hour and a quarter on the wheel, after having had his limbs crushed to pieces, hearing the indignant murmurs of an immense crowd which had assembled to see him suffer.

Sinister Forebodings

The public, always led into extremes, was persuaded that the two executed criminals were the leaders of a numerous band, organised for the most frightful purposes. This report derived some credit from a series of crimes that were discovered one after the other. The *valet-de-chambre* of a Lieutenant General, entrusted by his master to negotiate for 100,000 livres of shares, was found cut to pieces at the foot of the Pont Royal. In the night following the execution of Count de Horn, the watch discovered, near the Temple walls, a hired carriage half-upset, without horses or driver, in which was a bag filled with the body of a woman cut in pieces, who had been murdered, they said, after having been robbed of 300,000 livres in Banknotes. Five assassinations of this kind occurred during the following eight days. A quantity of arms, legs, and trunks of the corpses of people who had been assassinated and cut to pieces were dragged out of the river.

From Paris, the contagion of crime seemed to reach the Provinces. The roads, it was said, were infested with masked highwaymen who stopped the carriages. Histories, like the following, were tremblingly related. "On the 30th of March five officers, passing through the forest of Orleans, were attacked by a band of seventeen robbers. They defended themselves so vigorously that they killed eight of them; but the survivors having whistled, several more came up, so that the officers, having submitted, were cut to pieces and robbed. The Grand Provost of Paris was sent with some archers to scour the forest."

No doubt fear exaggerated things; but there was no illusion about melancholy accidents, cheatings, and other crimes too well proved. If some speculators punished themselves for their want of skill by suicide, the greater number among them fell into a kind of passion, and every means seemed good to them to retrieve themselves. Forgeries of paper became more and more frequent. A band of nine forgers was surprised, all clerks of notaries or attorneys. Bank clerks were arrested for embezzlement. They were obliged to organise companies of veterans, chosen with care, equipped and paid at great expense by the Indian Company, to replace the soldiers of the regiment of guards, who, until then, had been on guard at the doors and in the offices of the establishment, "because," we read in Buvat's Journal, "some were caught filching, picking the pockets of people who came to change their securities, of their Banknotes and silver."

Like the flocks which scent the storm, the people had a presentiment of political catastrophes. The imaginations of the populace, oppressed by a vague dread which they communicated to each other, saw everywhere sinister phenomena, warnings from above. Symptoms of this kind threw a gloom over the first months of 1720. Buvat, the passive echo of all current reports, naïvely tells us in his journal, that, near Corbeil, bands of wolves, issuing from the woods, had devoured many people: that the citizens of Rouen were in a state of alarm, because, during the first three days of March, they had seen the glare of a terrible fire which spread a thick and stinking smoke. Smallpox, which made frightful ravages, especially among the nobility, seemed equally a punishment from Heaven. Terrible phenomena appeared in the air: burning beams which became animated and took menacing shapes, or even extraordinarily luminous stars which suddenly spread out long arms. When such reports circulate among the populace, a crisis is certain to be at hand.

CHAPTER VII

THE FALL OF THE SCHEME

CHAPTER VII

THE FALL OF THE SCHEME

The Bank Reunited with the Indian Company

"Since Law has become Controller-General," said the Regent, "his head is turned." Indeed, from the day when the author of the *Scheme* was disconcerted by the movement of the realisers, it is very difficult to follow his operations; they are the headlong incoherent acts of a sinking man.

A meeting of the principal shareholders of the Company was convened for the 22nd of February at the office of the Bank. There assembled the Duke of Orleans, the Duke of Bourbon, many Princes, Dukes, and nobles, most of the Directors of the Company, and speculators, having large interests in the trade in shares, to the number of about two hundred. "These last," says Buvat, "were for the most part so superbly dressed, that the princes just named did not approach them in that respect." It was noticed as one of the miracles of stockjobbing, that upstarts, sprung from nothing, were found mixed up with princes, and brilliant enough to eclipse them.

The object of this meeting was the reunion of the Bank

and the Indian Company. On the Regent's proposal, the Royal Bank, becoming once more a simple branch of a private establishment, was again annexed to the Company; an operation of which they did not clearly perceive the bearing, since the King must remain responsible for the notes already issued, and the Bank was obliged to solicit the authority of power to create new securities.

The first impression of the public showed itself in a confidence which the least consideration ought to have dissipated. What, indeed, were they about to see? A Bank issuing paper to support a commercial enterprise, and this enterprise draining its receipts from the Bank to serve for capital. It was a monstrosity.

Financial Expedients

The Bank and the Company had not been united eight days before they were already obliged to have recourse to despotic and disastrous expedients to support this combination. On the 27th of February, the domiciliary visits began to seize, in the houses of private people, sums exceeding 500 livres in specie. The decree of the 5th of March was the signal for a kind of riot in the army of stockjobbers. This decree, comprising very various provisions, had for its object to restrain the circulation of paper, and to prevent the exaggerated rise of the shares. With strange inconsistency, Law, who had done his best to over-excite stockjobbing, now sought to stifle it in its expansion.

Orders were given to the treasurer of the Bank to call in, as they fell due, all sums advanced to speculators on the deposit of shares. The Company had not yet got in (or scarcely any of it) the enormous sum of 1,620 millions, arising from the last shares created, at 5,000 livres each: as yet only four payments had been made by the subscribers. According to the terms of the decree of the 5th of March, the receipts for these last payments were to be received in deduction of the sums lent by the Bank—a combination which tended to reduce the number of shares. The saleable value of the shares was fixed at 9,000 livres; and, in spite of the engagement undertaken eight days earlier, two offices were opened for the conversion, at the will of the holders, of Banknotes into shares, and shares into Banknotes, at the rate of 9,000 livres. The last articles regulated the currency of metallic money at the price of ninety livres to the silver marc. This new reduction artificially multiplied the specie, so as to make it suffice for the reimbursement of the paper.

The advances made by the Bank to speculators amounted to 450 millions. If Law had imposed on its debtors the obligation of paying in Banknotes, he might have saved the *Scheme*. In fact, the notes in circulation then amounted to 1,100 millions. The sudden withdrawal of 450 millions would have raised to par, and, doubtless, above, the credit paper, which began to be depreciated. But in thus acting, Law would have "sold up" a great number of speculators, and especially many very great nobles, whom he would have made his mortal enemies. He dared not take this violent course; and received in payment, as we have just seen, the portion already paid up on the shares subscribed for. This proceeding cancelled the investment of nearly the whole of the shares issued at 5,000 livres. Law pursued the following reasoning on this subject: a considerable number of shares being cancelled, the dividend to divide among the classed shares will be so considerable, that everybody will wish to invest his disposable capital in the Company. With this persuasion he fancied that the shares offered at the fixed price of 9,000 livres would be so much the more sought after, as they would preserve the right of conversion without losing the share in money, or the money in shares. But distrust, infused like poison into the veins of society, had already become an incurable disease. The purchase office became a desert; the office of sale was besieged. Most of the shareholders converted their shares into notes, and realised, at any price, either by selling their shares at a loss for silver, or by sending the notes into the provinces, where payments were not suspended; or, lastly, by buying at excessive prices goods of all kinds.

This exchange, in open office, of shares for notes at the price of 9,000 livres, brought about a new issue of paper at a time when it was necessary to reduce its circulation. There was but one means of preventing its entire destruction: this was absolutely to suppress the use of coined money. Thence that fatal and ridiculous declaration of the 11th of March, tending to proscribe gold money absolutely, and to restrain the use of silver to the small pieces.

Stockjobbing is Forbidden

The convulsive movements of expiring stockjobbing counteracted these new measures of the government. The dreadful affair of the Count de Horn furnished a pretext for forbidding the meetings in the Rue Quincampoix. The decree, already prepared, was proclaimed by sound of trumpet on the 22nd of March, the day of the crime, to the great satisfaction of the peaceful inhabitants of the district. The famous street, so noisy and so blocked up before, became suddenly as melancholy and deserted as a cursed spot.

It was, nevertheless, a strange inconsistency to reduce all the securities of a country to negotiable paper, and forbid its negotiation. From force of circumstances, speculators then met in the neighbourhood of the Bank, especially the Place des Victoires, and addressed one another to speak on business. The group increased in a few moments; the news related, the demand and the offers regulated the current prices. People bought at a premium in spite of the prohibition; calculations were made, discounts given, millions changed hands, until the cry was heard of "the watch! the watch!" Immediately every one took to flight to escape the blows of the flat of the sabres, which the mounted archers loved to bestow on the wandering stockjobbers. Thus, for two months, was carried on the dealings in paper.

A False Manoeuvre—Financial rout

To render transactions easier with the only currency they wished to preserve, a decree of the 19th of April ordered the division of notes of 10,000 into sums of 1,000 livres and under, and the manufacture of 438 millions of new notes of different values, from 1,000 livres to ten livres. To make notes still reimbursable as low as ten livres, was running ahead of a catastrophe.

There was a vague talk among the public of new combinations of the Controller-General to bring, within proper limits, the amount of notes in circulation, and to balance them against the commercial value of the shares, when, to the general astonishment, appeared the decree of the 21st of May. After an emphatic summary of the benefits of the *Scheme*, it was declared that the shares should undergo a successive diminution from month-to-month until the 1st of December, when they would remain fixed at 5,500 livres; that the Banknotes should be reduced in the same manner down to half their actual value. Nevertheless, the said notes were still to be received in their full value until the end of the year, in payment of taxes and in the acquisition of life annuities. As for bills of exchange and commercial engagements, the payments must be made in Banknotes, valued according to the legal rate at the time of the falling due. Lastly, it was given to be understood that the use of metallic money was about to be allowed, and that their intrinsic value would be increased two-thirds, by returning the money at the rate of thirty livres to the silver marc.

The partisans of Law allege that this decree was prepared in secret among the *coterie* of d'Argenson, and promulgated without the knowledge of the Controller-General. The enemies of the *Scheme*, on the contrary, give us long dissertations to throw on Law the responsibility of what the public considered a bankruptcy. The contest which ensued on this subject shows that the decree of the 21st of May was never properly understood.

Before this decree, a share of 9,000 livres at ninety livres the marc, produced one hundred marcs of silver (or 25 kilogrammes). After this decree, a share reduced to 5,500 livres at thirty livres the marc, would have given, on the contrary, 183 marcs (or more than 45 kilogrammes). Instead of a bankruptcy, there would have been a profit to the shareholder of nearly 100 percent. This combination bears too much of the impress of Law's speculative genius for us to doubt that he was the author of it.

The intention was honest; but its execution appeared chimerical to calculators. The multitude, who do not reason, were struck by the word "reduction," and cried out "robbery—bankruptcy." The Duke de Bourbon added fire and flames, and it is said that they could only appease him by giving him four millions. The price of provisions immediately rose to an extent which gave rise to much apprehension. From Paris, the irritation spread to the Provinces. Riots were feared, and for many days the troops were kept in readiness.

This crisis lasted a week: the decree of the 21st was revoked by another decree of the 27th. The note and the share recovered the value they had previously had. The remedy was more dangerous than the disease. The decree of the 21st of May had knocked down the *Scheme*: that of the 27th gave it the death-blow.

The least clear-sighted understood that papers, whose value might be increased or diminished, by one-half by decree, were a slight guarantee under an absolute government. The grand affair for each family was to secure some portion of its capital. Some fell into a sombre despair: others consoled themselves by singing to the air of *les Pendus*, (the hanged), this apropos ditty:—

> *On Monday, I bought some shares;*
> *On Tuesday, I gained millions;*
> *On Wednesday, I furnished my house;*
> *On Thursday, I started a carriage;*
> *On Friday, I went to a ball;*
> *And on Saturday to the Hospital.*

The animosity against Law burst forth with such strength that he was obliged to resign his office of Superintendent of Finance; for they had revived this title for him, which had been suppressed since Fouquet's disgrace. The Regent demanded of him his accounts, and placed a guard of Swiss guards over him. People considered him lost. In reality it was done to preserve him from the fury of the populace. Besides, he was retained in his essential office of Director of the Indian Company, with a seat in the Council of the Regency.

Still, many decrees which followed one another rapidly were considered by the public as a repudiation of the *Scheme*. Especially the prohibition against coining gold, and that against possessing more than 500 livres in silver were revoked. This alternation inspired the citizens with the following melancholy reflection recorded in *Barbier's Journal*:—"There is a decree which allows us to have as much money in our houses as we please. This permission comes when nobody has got any!"

The urgent affair, the measure of safety, consisted in reducing the frightful mass of paper in circulation, by offering to annuitants the chance of retaining some sort of income. After an official examination of the balance sheet of the Company, it was seen that, by cancelling the 300,000 shares bought up, and the 100,000 possessed by the King, they could reduce the number of the others to 200,000, secure to the shares preserved an interest of 3 percent, bind the shareholders of the new society to a payment of 3,000 livres per share, payable in credit paper, so as to reduce the mass: lastly, to raise annuities on the Hotel de Ville at the rate of 40 percent, to procure employment for the Banknotes, and for the reimbursement of receipts. The result of this last operation was, that annuitants who received 4 and 5 percent before being reimbursed, would be forced to reinvest their capital at 2 and one-half percent: it was a partial bankruptcy.

The Account at the Bank

Another expedient, proposed for diminishing the floating mass of notes, might have been efficacious if confidence had not at this period been irrevocably lost. Merchants were invited to deposit in the Bank, or its branches, a sum of notes proportioned to the extent of their transactions. By means of these accounts current, the Bank would have effected, without expense, all commercial payments by simple transfers in writing. But the exchange of a discredited paper was no longer a sufficient guarantee for commercial transactions. Instead of the 600 millions of notes which they hoped to absorb by means of the accounts current, the deposits scarcely reached a third of that sum.

These decrees, upsetting existing things from morning till night, had caused a kind of stupefaction among the public. They no longer tried to distinguish the good from the evil: it was an "everyone for himself," in which everyone strove to recover a little of the metal so heroically despised the previous year. Besides, the conversion of paper into cash was likely to be a Herculean labour. The Bank, in the month of June, could pay no more than ten livres note to each person. The master of the house, who wanted one hundred livres, sent ten different persons, and so there was a crowd which rendered the counters unapproachable. This circumstance made a new kind of stockjobbers spring up. The market carriers and porters discounted, at a low price, the small notes of timid citizens, and they had done a good day's work when they had received the ten livres at the Bank. But before reaching the counter, what cries, oaths, and blows were exchanged! To venture into such a crush one ought to have been a gladiator.

The Camp of the Place Vendôme

The more rapid the decline of the paper was, the greater was the desire for speculation. By remonstrances and prayers the stockjobbers obtained permission to continue their trade publicly. The Place Vendôme was assigned to them as a place of meeting. The aspect of this new exchange in the open air was very different to that of the Rue Quincampoix. It was the 2nd of June. An excessive heat obliged the dealers to have several rows of tents erected. Some served for offices of business; others, more spacious and elegant, were places of refreshment and pleasure. There soon reappeared speculators from all the French Provinces, and from all the nations of Europe, who added to this picture the exciting variety of costumes and accents. Games and lotteries were tolerated there. Curiosity and fashion drew the great ladies there, and also many adventuresses. All this was gay and lively, and in no way recalled the brutal avidity of the Rue Quincampoix.

These tents, in symmetrical rows, bore, at a short distance, the appearance of a camp on the day after a victory. This resemblance gave satirists the idea of placarding, at the four corners of the place, a pretended order of the day, bearing pointed allusion to persons compromised in the *Scheme*.

Although the shares were still kept up to 5,000 livres in Banknotes, the real business in hand was to regulate the commercial course of the paper in relation to money and other effectual securities. The large notes, very difficult to get rid of, lost 25 to 50 percent; they were exchanged at this price, not for silver but for goods of value. In each tent were bought or sold jewels, plate, furniture, and rich stuffs. The Place Vendôme resembled one of those rich bazaars described in the "Thousand and One Nights." The principal articles of trade were precious stones and pearls, which reached fabulous prices; large quantities of these soon came into France, so that in spite of the prohibition against wearing them, many persons displayed in the place of meeting, even in the streets, an oriental extravagance. Perceiving in this fashion danger to the public fortune and injury to morals, the government withdrew the special permissions which it had previously given, and forbade, absolutely, the trade in, and use of, precious stones, under pain of confiscation and a fine of 10,000 livres.

Another sort of trade which government could not tolerate was the exchange, at a loss, of notes for silver, or the purchase of pieces of money according to their intrinsic value. How could it give and receive these securities at a legal par, if it allowed them to be publicly negotiated at a price below what it had arbitrarily assigned to them? In spite of the threat of being sent to the galleys, people escaped its vigilance by all sorts of tricks; and, in the end, the depreciated notes and debased coins were exchanged almost publicly, following the changes which public confidence impressed on them. This notorious discredit of the legal money was death to the *Scheme*. One fine day the police drove the brokers from the Place Vendôme, whip in hand, like the traders from the Temple, and a place was prepared for these negotiations where authority could exercise its control with efficacy.

Chapter VII

Court Intrigues

In the midst of these unruly proceedings, Law's position had become a very dangerous one. The Duke de Broglie, who pretended to be a physiognomist and a plain speaker, had dared to say at the Regent's table, and, while looking the Director of the Bank straight in the face, that he would end with a halter. It was publicly bet on the London Exchange that the hanging would take place in the month of September. Law himself, with all his courage, felt fear, and did not conceal it. He dreaded lest some court intrigue or street riot should put a tragic end to his experiment. "I am like," he said, "a hen laying golden eggs, who, when dead, would be worth no more than a common hen."

He was, in fact, on a slippery declivity, at the foot of which his enemies were digging an abyss. The authors of the *Anti-Scheme*, the brothers Paris, creatures of the Chancellor d'Argenson, attempted everything against him which hatred and the genius of intrigue could devise. But to hang Law the concurrence of Parliament would have been needed; and, once launched into political action, the Parliament might have chosen to proclaim the King's majority, give him a royal council, and perhaps arrest the Regent. Probably it was this that saved the Scotchman. The Regent, who besides liked him, was interested in not abandoning him. On the 2nd of July, d'Argenson and his son were removed from their posts. The four brothers Paris received orders to retire to Dauphiny. As a concession to public opinion, Law advised the recall of d'Aguesseau, exiled to his estate at Fresne, went to fetch him himself, and persuaded him to return and replace the old d'Argenson as Chancellor.

The Battles of the Rue Vivienne

From day to day and hour to hour, the scenes which took place before the doors of the Bank became more alarming. "The day before yesterday, 5th June," says Barbier, "there was a fearful fray, and swords drawn. The soldiers twice fixed bayonets to their guns. Scarcely anything is needed to set sedition in a blaze." They attempted to divide this focus of sedition by increasing the exchange offices. Notice was given to the public, that in future the division of notes of one hundred livres into notes of ten livres, and the conversion of these notes of ten livres into money, would be made on market days, that is, twice a-week, at the houses of the eight district Commissaries.

To promise money on market days, was to offer bread to the starving; for the small traders and dealers being obliged to receive the ten livres notes in payment, were literally exposed to perish of hunger, with paper which they could not use for retail purchases. In spite of strong files of soldiers of the guards, which were tripled on the days of distribution, there were at each Commissary's door the same blockade, the same violence, the same despair, as at the door of the Bank. The emotions of the crowd still palpitate in the MS. journals of the time:—"The distributors," says the advocate Barbier, "are at present like little ministers; for magistrates, and people of the highest rank, go and beg of them as a favour to keep 100 livres on their account, because they only give 10 livres to the populace; it is a regular slaughter on Wednesdays and Saturdays. Nobody really has any money, and it seems that they go to ask for charity." In what old Buvat writes, we see the bad temper of a man coming home at night after having been crushed and knocked about, perhaps without any result:—"The door was only half open, so that the money seekers should only enter one by one, and none got in but the strongest. Most of them brought away nothing but sweat and fatigue instead of money, because the preference that the Commissaries gave to their friends had exhausted the funds, and they reserved a portion for themselves."

The Commissaries, each of whom had but 20,000 to 30,000

livres to dispense on each day of distribution, could not satisfy everyone. Besieged by the entreaties of great people, and alarmed at the increasing exasperation of the lower orders, they declared that they could no longer answer for the public safety. They were, therefore, relieved from their unpleasant office, which did not last more than a month.

Circulation of money being suspended, it was necessary that something should be done for the subsistence of the people. They did not trouble themselves about the means. They converted into money the notes presented by the Paris bakers. The bakers of the suburbs, who partly provisioned the capital, received premiums to continue their supply. Four hundred thousand livres per week were distributed for the market of Poissy, and 50,000 livres for the poultry market. Large sums of money were placed at the disposal of the heads of manufactures to pay their salaries.

On closing the offices of the Commissaries, it was announced that the Bank would exchange alternatively the large notes for small ones, and the small ones for money. To economise the cash, the offices were only opened from morning till mid-day. Only one note of ten livres was paid to each person, and very slowly, so that half the people, arrived ever since the night previous, returned home worn out with fatigue, wearied by the excessive heat, dying of hunger, and without having obtained anything.

The Rue Vivienne was a kind of field of battle where the dead and wounded were daily picked up. On the 5th of July, stones having been thrown in the gardens of the Mazarin Palace, twenty soldiers charged with fixed bayonets against a thick crowd. On the following days several persons were stifled to death. On the 10th, a servant, sent by his master, tried to enter before his turn; a soldier struck him to the earth with a blow of his gun. At this act of cruelty, the crowd collected in the street was exasperated; they hurled showers of stones into the courtyard of the Mazarin Palace, where there were not soldiers but private individuals already admitted to the inside, and waiting their turn at the door of the office. Many of these were wounded. At the same time the guard on duty took up a defensive position, and made a bloody sortie against the assailants.

Sedition

The capital poured out drop by drop by the Bank soon disappeared. The smallest salaries being often paid in paper, with which those little purchases which fed a poor household could not be made, it was absolutely necessary for these miserable people, sometimes old men or mothers of families, to come, at the peril of their lives, to try and get silver. The crowd increasing every day, as well as the seriousness of the accidents, the Bank conceived the unlucky idea of having a palisade erected in front of the door, forming a narrow passage; it was a means of retarding the crowd. On the 17th of July, the number of persons who stationed themselves in the Rue Vivienne and Rue des Petits Champs, from three o'clock in the morning, was reckoned at fifteen thousand. Then arrived those bands of brutal men who made a trade of changing the notes. Impatient at the obstacle they met with, they mounted on the palings, and threw themselves at full length in the crowd, already jammed together in the passage. Dreadful groans of pain soon burst forth, mingled with the cries of some from fear, and others from indignation. It was equally impossible to get away or to render assistance, the crowd was so dense. At length they managed, at about five in the morning, to clear away this heap of human beings. Sixteen people were taken out dead or dying.

This time the people lost patience; their anger burst forth in cries of rage, which resounded even to the remotest quarters. The tumult assumed the character of an insurrection: the corpses were placed on litters; five of them were marched up the Rue Vivienne; three were taken towards the Palais Royal. The crowd formed a procession crying out for vengeance; they excited themselves by singing some of those seditious verses which had been placarded about for some days, such as this, to an air then in vogue:—

> *Frenchmen, courage fails you,*
> *You are full of blindness:*
> *To hang Law with the Regent,*
> *And seize the Bank,*
> *Is but the affair of a moment!*

It was about six o'clock in the morning when the three corpses, carried to the Palais Royal, were deposited at the door. "The people followed in a fury, and tried to enter the palace, which was immediately closed on every side. They were assured that the Regent was at Bagnolet. The people replied, that that was not true; that they had but to set fire to the four corners of the building and they would find him. Soon there was a frightful riot in the district. One band carried a corpse to the Louvre; another band rushed off to Law's house, where they broke all the windows.[1]

Although brave, the Regent was in great alarm. The exasperation of the riotous crowd was founded on so legitimate a cause, it was so completely in harmony with the general feeling, that they dared not set on the troops, many corps of whom were not to be depended on. The Minister of War, and the Governor of Paris, showed themselves at their windows, descended to the Place, preached moderation, distributed money, and thus

---

1. Buvat

gained three hours. During this time the officers of the Prince had dressed up musketeers and soldiers of the guard as private citizens, and had introduced them into the palace. A double increase of vociferations and threats being heard about nine o'clock, the gates were opened and many thousands of persons rushed into the courtyard, when the gate was again closed on them. The oblong court was surrounded and commanded on all sides by high buildings pierced with windows. A portion of the assailants finding themselves blocked in this place, the disturbance became less threatening.

Another event added also to the popular indignation. In a carriage turning the corner of the Rue Croix des Petits Champs, and entering the Rue St. Honoré, a woman recognised the Director of the Bank. This unfortunate creature had just heard of the death of her husband, who had been stifled in the morning. She stopped the horses by seizing their bridles, and cried out "Vengeance!" Law sprang out, and recovering his old duellist's presence of mind, coolly said to those who were attacking him, "You are a set of scum," (*vous êtes des canailles.*) Whether the expression was lost in the noise, or that his majestic coolness awed the crowd, the Scotchman managed to reach the Palais Royal without accident. Again surrounded on leaving the palace, the coachman in his turn assumed the grand airs of his master, and said from his seat on high, "You are a set of scum;" so much the worse for him. He was immediately thrown to the earth, pounded with blows, and carried away dying. The carriage he was driving was smashed to pieces.

"It was a wonder," says St. Simon, "how Paris got quiet again, and did not revolt altogether, and at once." A burlesque incident shows, in fact, that sedition was lurking in all classes. During the crisis, the grand chamber of Parliament was holding its morning audience at the Palais de Justice. The first president, De Mesme, having had occasion to leave the room for a moment, learnt what had happened on the other bank of the Seine. He reentered the room in haste, and taking a theatrical attitude in the midst of the assembled senate, he cried out:—

Messieurs, Messieurs, good news increases—
The carriage of Law is smashed to pieces.[2]

This impromptu was soon celebrated. It is true that the first president was a member of the French Academy.

Coup d'état—Banishment of the Parliament

There was still disturbance; but the imminent danger had passed, when the friends of the Regent, those young nobles who gloried in the name *roués*, arrived at the Palais Royal. They came from a nocturnal orgie which had been held at the residence of one of them in a small house at the Faubourg St. Antoine: a sort of council was formed. The unanimous opinion was, that the spark of sedition was still smouldering; and that it only needed the Parliament to stir the ashes, and a conflagration would burst forth. They, therefore, considered themselves justified in preventing such an explosion by a little *coup d'état*.

Troops were brought towards Paris: a camp was formed at Charenton. An order was given to the musketeers and archers of the watch to remain under arms, and ready to march at a moment's notice. Law was concealed in the Palais Royal, where he remained ten days. At length, to neutralise public opinion, they distributed by hawkers a notice thus worded:—"The Parliament, by its constant opposition to Government, keeps back the silver; but in spite of its evil intention, the silver will

---

2. The original contains an allusion and a pun, which are untranslatable, and a round-about explanation of a joke always spoils it—so I will not attempt it.—Translator.

appear next week, and the Banknote will no longer lose in change."

The Parliament took its revenge. All the evil arising from the depreciation of the Banknotes, the Indian Company had offered to take them up and extinguish them at fifty millions a month for a year, provided the commercial privileges on which its existence rested were renewed in perpetuity. This offer, being calculated to restore credit, had been agreed to by Government and converted into a decree. The public were pleased with it; the Parliament obstinately refused its adhesion. For some time there had been much talk of plans concerted between Law and Dubois, tending to suppress the supreme courts, after having given compensation to all the appointments and judicial offices depending on them. They would have instituted a magistracy nominated by the King and removable from office, in place of the parliamentary judges, who, having acquired a property in their places, had a sort of independence. Such a project being only practicable by means of the resources furnished by the Indian Company, the members of the Parliament had very little sympathy for measures calculated to strengthen the *Scheme*. Therefore they refused to register the edict which, while saving the Bank, would have perpetuated the Company.

This refusal was necessarily unpopular, and gave the Regent an advantage. On the 21st of July, before eight o'clock in the morning, the Palais de Justice was suddenly invaded by several bodies of troops. The King's house was divided into inner halls. The French guards ranged themselves in fighting order on the grand staircase and in the courtyards. The Swiss guards kept the passages. The foot and mounted watch patrolled the district in companies. At the same time, musketeers going and arousing the presidents and councillors of the Parliament, gave them an order of banishment to Pontoise.

So many precautions were superfluous. The Parliament was

no longer in a humour to resist, nor of a character to excite much regret. The shares of the Company rose at once from 4,560 livres to 5,700 livres. The sixteen presidents, the seventy-two councillors, the bar, followed by an army of recorders, advocates, attorneys, officers and pleaders, prepared for the outset without whispering a word against it. For many days the streets leading to the Pontoise road were blocked up with wagons full of furniture; and, from time to time, were heard these verses which translated well enough the sole interests of the moment.

> *The Parliament is at Pontoise*
> *Sur Oise*
> *By the Regent's command:*
> *But will they return our money to hand?*
> *No! It is only to get up a noise*
> *With the Parliament,*
> *Which is going to sleep at Pontoise*
> *Sur Oise,*
> *By the Regent's order sent.*

The day after the *coup d'état* they were able to send the troops back to their quarters. The musketeers alone remained bivouacked in the palace. What could they do in the sanctuary of justice, but pass judgment? "To amuse themselves, the young ones played at 'Parliament.' One was made first president, others presidents, King's counsel, and advocates. Meanwhile, having received some sausages and a pie for breakfast, they pronounced sentence, condemning the sausages to the fire, and the pie to be broken." This was a summary and urgent judgment; but next day, a cat having committed a fault, judgment was executed on her with all ceremony.

Hearing of these unseemly proceedings, and excesses of

other kinds committed in the grand chamber, the principal seat of kingly justice, the exiles at Pontoise exclaimed against the scandal. But did these magistrates themselves preserve that severe dignity which is a homage to the sanctity of the law? The advocate Marias thus writes, on his return from the journey to Pontoise. "We did nothing here but eat and drink, play at a frightful rate, which ruins all the young folks, and hang a few criminals here and there." Saint-Simon lets us into the secret of this joyous life. The first president, De Mesme, not very well regarded among his own sect, conceived the idea of a reconciliation with it, while at the same time paying his court to the Duke of Orleans. Having insinuated to the Prince that it would be good policy to lessen the parliamentary opposition, by sweetening the bitterness of their exile, he received more than 100,000 crowns, with which he managed to feast and amuse his colleagues so well, that on seeing them anyone would have taken them, not for banished senators, but lawyer's clerks out for a holiday.

Dearness of Merchandise—Embassy of the Six Corps

In Paris the financial crisis raged worse than ever. Provisions, forcibly exchanged for debased paper, attained excessive prices. From July to October bread was sold at four to five sous the pound, and meat in proportion. Candles, although fixed at the maximum of ten sous the pound, cost thirty-two sous. Articles of luxury were rendered doubly dear, both by the depreciation of the circulating medium, and by the emptiness of the shops. A pound of coffee cost eighteen livres instead of fifty sous, a pair of silk stockings forty livres, an ell of fine cloth eighty livres. Stuffs reached at last such insupportable prices, that there was a regular concert of complaints, not only among the public, but on the part of the clothing contractors, who declared that they could no longer supply clothes to the troops. The Indian

Company perceived danger to itself in these recriminations. What could it do? Persuaded, probably, that traders raise their prices from malice, it determined to oppose them by competition. Having made a contract with the manufacturer Van Robais for the purchase of a considerable quantity of cloth, it offered to clothe the soldiers at the ordinary prices; and, still more, it opened a warehouse to the public, where were found working tailors in its pay, who made clothes to measure at moderate prices.

Such an attempt on the part of so enterprising a company was calculated to alarm the citizens. Was the *Scheme* then going to invade private industry? Such a report was spread, and it had a marked effect on trade. The drapers instituted against the house of Van Robais one of those law suits which then lasted a quarter of a century. The citizens themselves, represented by the six corps of tradesmen,[3] thought right to interfere, and it was agreed that the masters and keepers of the merchandise should proceed as a deputation to the Chief of the State. On the appointed day the thirty-six masters and keepers, dressed in their finest clothes and most official wigs, marched in procession through the streets of Paris towards the Palais Royal. Unfortunately, the Duke of Orleans had been forewarned of it: he was persuaded that the exorbitant price of goods was the result of a culpable avarice and a plot against the *Scheme*. Before the orator of the six corps had time to state their troubles, the Regent shut his mouth by crying —"You are a set of thieves, robbers, and ungovernable beings." Then, turning his back to them, he sent them off with a bit of Billingsgate, a modest translation of which would be—"Go about your business!" Imagine the open-mouthed amazement of the gentlemen of the

---

3. The six corps comprised drapers, grocers, mercers, furriers, hosiers, and goldsmiths, with accessory trades. Each corp nominated six masters and keepers to watch over the preservation of their statutes and privileges.

six corps at these coarse words! A thunderbolt falling in the midst of them would not have caused more horror.

The unanimous advice was to go at once and lay a complaint before the King. The King, alas, was only nine years old. His governor, the Duke de Villeroi, received them in place of him. This old nobleman aspired to represent the grand and noble manners of the former reign. He behaved with finished politeness: but all they could extract from him was, that the allegation was "improbable, impossible"—they must have misunderstood. More than once, the worthy citizens glanced at one another; the coarse word had vibrated in their ears, so that there could be no mistake about it. Despairing of their case, they went to the Chancellor, M. d'Aguesseau. "My lord," added they, after having explained the facts, "when the six corps have the honour of being admitted by the King or the Regent, they are accustomed to inscribe on the register the words that the Chief of the State deigns to address to them. Will you be kind enough to tell us what we ought to do today?" d'Aguesseau, who was a grave man, clinging to traditions, advised them to draw up their record as usual, at the same time trying to soften things a little.

Exasperation—Threats

The dearness increasing from day to day, the sustenance of life, eating and drinking, had become difficult problems even to the distinguished classes. Imagine then the degree of uneasiness and exasperation to which those had reached who lived from hand to mouth. From time to time they pillaged the provincial markets—disorders which were inevitably followed by a kind of dearth. In Paris, the uneasiness showed itself in peculiar and entirely local symptoms: it was an increase of songs, satires, placards, and caricatures, printed, engraved, or in manuscript. The provocation was even displayed in medals. The town was literally inundated with these things. "For the last few days," writes the advocate Barbier, "engraved notes have been thrown into carriages, in which it is said— 'Save the King, kill the tyrant, don't trouble yourself about the disturbance.'" Another of the most violent *tocsins* was so multiplied, that thirty manuscript copies of it were found in the Palais Royal alone. The mocking Parisian vein was no longer to be discovered in these writings, they breathed a spirit of insurrection. If a paper fastened to a wall attracted notice, something of this sort was sure to be found in it:—

> *John Law has merited the cord,*
> *The Regent has deserved the sword;*
> *And hence the concord comes to pass,*
> *Twist the Regent and this Monsieur Lass.*

The post carried everywhere the same anonymous threats. "I have received," says the Regent's mother, in her memoirs, "letters in which frightful threats are made against my son, assuring me that two hundred bottles of poisoned wine have been prepared for him; and that, if that should fail, a new sort of fire work would be used to burn my son alive in the Palais Royal, and myself here at St. Cloud." Three separate times the Princess speaks of similar letters.

The Pamphleteers

The Duke of Orleans, though proud and rash, was scarcely revengeful; he readily despised injuries and threats. Nevertheless, there was one piece which touched him on a tender point, alluding to a design, which slanderers attributed to him, of poisoning Louis XV to usurp his crown. It was a parody on the last scene of *Mithridates*, in which the Regent is supposed to be dying of a wound received during a rebellion, and opening his heart at the last moment to his two accomplices, Law and the Duke of Bourbon. It will be sufficient to quote four lines to show its tone:—

> *Heav'n has not willed that, favouring my design,*
> *The King should die through poisoned cup of mine:*
> *But still one joy consoles me in my death—*
> *'Mid robb'd annuitants I yield my breath.*

One day the Regent found this piece fastened to the door of his closet. He was wounded to the quick; and in the evening, while relating the fact to six of his most devoted courtiers, who assisted at his going to bed, he added: "I would give a hundred thousand crowns to discover the author." The next morning another piece of paper, fastened in the same place, attracted his notice, and he read on it this distich:—

> *Regent, you promise much to pay!*
> *But is't in paper, or silver, pray?*

This anecdote having given importance to the parody, the public would have the name of the author to cite, and persisted, against probability, in attributing it to the poet Vergier, a commissary of the navy, a rich man, and an agreeable rhymer, who, having had some acquaintance with La Fontaine in his youth, was considered in society as his disciple. He was then sixty-three years old. On the 23rd of August, on coming from a dinner at one of his friends, "Vergier was followed by an assassin, who, coming up to him in the Rue du Bout du Monde, said to him, '*It's you, then, Vergier, the Magnificent?*' and at the same time fired a pistol at him. As this gentleman was still breathing, the assassin finished killing him by several bayonet thrusts, and then saved himself by flight. The watch coming up, they carried the body to the morgue of the Châtelet, dressed in brown cloth, with gold lace three inches wide, and a waistcoat of gold brocade. His heirs laid information of the assassination—and, nevertheless, the affair was pursued no farther by superior orders."[4] To this account of Buvat, Marais adds that Vergier had money about him, some notes, and a watch, and that he was not robbed. A scoundrel of Cartouche's band, executed in 1722, was accused of this crime, and threw the odium of it on two police agents, named Leroux and Bourdon. However it might be, the police were persuaded that the Regent wished to intimidate libellers from time to time by examples of this kind.

Cancelling of the Paper

In the midst of these agitations, the Government was evidently aiming at the eventual suppression of the paper, and the resumption of payments in specie. The administrative measures and financial decrees which followed one another without interruption till the month of October, are like palliations to soothe the pain of the transition.

The Indian Company was reorganised by confining it within the proportions of a simple commercial society, independent of the State. Banknotes were periodically burned. At several times life annuities were created at 4 percent, and perpetual annuities at 2 percent, so as to open outlets for the large notes, till the 5th of October. It was ordered that the small notes should cease to

---

4. Extract from Buvat's MS. Journal. In the same collection, at a little later date (April, 1722), we read:—"A man named Sandrier, first clerk of the Treasurer of war, and a novelist, was found in the river, pierced with two dagger wounds. It is said that it was for speaking ill of the government."

have currency after the 1st of May of the following year. It was allowed to be stipulated in contracts that payments should only be made in money. A little later, it was decreed that notes could only be given in payment with half in specie; that the sums deposited in the Bank, under the head of current accounts, would in future only be reckoned at one-fourth of their nominal value; that the shares of the Indian Company would in future be valued at the rate of 2,000 livres. By degrees the intrinsic value of the coinage was raised. Onerous obligations were imposed on shareholders, so as to be able to visit with forfeiture those who did not conform to them.

At last, on the 10th of October, appeared a celebrated decree, which, after deduction of the notes created and cancelled, definitively called on the holders to lay out those which remained in their hands before the 1st of November, either in perpetual annuities at 2 percent, or in life annuities at 4 percent, or in the capital of the new Indian Company.

The Hotel de Soissons

The fall of all credit securities was hastened by the stockjobbers, who, having turned their batteries, now played for a fall in a manner calculated to inspire despair among that portion of the public who were forced to exchange actual property for paper. Since the Place Vendôme had been cleared, whip in hand, the principal seat of stockjobbing had been established in the garden of the Hotel des Soissons, on the spot where the corn-market has since been built. The Prince de Carignau, the proprietor of this hotel, had granted to some speculators, for 150,000 livres per annum, the right of erecting some wooden sheds intended for the stockjobbers. One hundred and thirty-eight boxes, raised as if by enchantment, and well ornamented, were immediately let at the exorbitant price of 500 livres the month. The opening of this new Exchange took place on the

1st of August with some sort of ceremony, and to the sound of military music. "I have been to see the traders in paper in their boxes," writes the advocate Marais in his Memorial; "there are some who have pretty wives with them, and the latter do more business than the others."

The number of professional stockjobbers being limited by the number of boxes, it was thought that an influence might be exercised over them which would be useful to credit. The coinage had first been again debased by being valued at 120 livres to the silver marc. The notes being half their value, it was thought that they might be placed on a par with the silver, by taking away from the latter half its value. Thanks to this deplorable expedient, the brokers of the Hotel De Soissons for some days exchanged the ten livres notes at par. But to attempt to stop the fall of a debased currency is to strive against a torrent. In spite of the police, the paper was taken for what it was worth; the debased coins were only sold by weight. Not only did the trade in precious articles spring up again at the Hotel de Soissons, but quantities of furniture and clothes were brought there, which gave the Exchange the appearance of a market. This became a useless scandal from the day when the Government resolved to forbid the circulation of the paper. On the 29th of October, the doors of the Hotel de Soissons were closed by order of the Government. A prohibition was made against meeting in any other place for the traffic in paper, under pain of imprisonment, and a fine of 3,000 livres. The mounted watch again began to give chase after the stockjobbers.

The Maximum

As the Banknotes were to cease to have forced currency from the 1st of November, it was natural that the shopkeepers should hesitate to receive them. Some only took them at a loss of 80 percent; others would not have them at any price. The repugnance for paper was shown in the Provinces even more energetically than in Paris. At Strasbourg there was a riot of the citizens and the garrison, both agreeing to reject the notes: at Lyons they sacked the offices of the Bank. Still could they condemn consumers to die of hunger who could offer nothing but notes since their silver had all been confiscated. Government took the part of the latter, and there was a two-fold increase of severity in the edicts against forestallers.

Eighteen Paris bakers, guilty of not choosing to sell at a loss, were sentenced to a fine, exposed for three market days with the iron collar[5] on, and ruined by the confiscation of their stocks in trade. A sentence of the Lieutenant of Police condemned "the man named Bouron and two other tallow-chandlers of the Rue St. Jacques to a fine of 500 livres, the said Bouron to have his shop closed for a month for refusing to sell candles to the public, though they had plenty in stock." The supply of wood failed, and the want of materials for fire at the beginning of winter was one of the things most dreaded in families accustomed to comfort. Not only were the dealers in wood proceeded against with lawsuits, but many private persons having been informed against as forestallers, the aldermen caused all the wood and coal to be sold belonging to those in whose houses they found supplies beyond their presumed consumption.

Decline of the Indian Company

Public anger growled secretly against those who had started the follies of the *Scheme*. An event, which was much talked about, led to a regular explosion. A certain man, named Vernezobre, a Prussian by birth, who had been originally an inferior clerk at the Bank, had become at length one of its principal cashiers; his duties having placed him in a position to play a safe game,

---

5. An ancient species of punishment like our stocks.—Translator.

he realised considerable sums in crown-pieces, jewels, and good bills of exchange, and set to work to convey it all to a foreign country. Lastly, the cashier himself followed his treasure.

Among the public, where even the great sou pieces were rare, the sum carried away by the Prussian adventurer was reckoned at fifty millions. This contrast provoked an outbreak of indignation with which authority armed itself to make those who were supposed to have been enriched by the *Scheme* give up their prey. It was forbidden, under the severest penalties, to leave the kingdom without special authority. The seizure of 77,000 louis d'or of twenty to the marc, (3,140,000 francs of the present day), made at the house of another cashier of the Bank, rendered all the people employed in that establishment suspected. Many of them were thrown into prison. A new call of capital, and other vexatious and onerous conditions for shareholders, so discouraged the holders of these securities, that they at last began to offer for a louis of forty-two livres, a share which had perhaps been purchased in the Rue Quincampoix at the price of 20,000 livres. At length the last blow was given to the Company's reputation by cancelling the contracts, which gave it the profits of coining money and the collection of the State revenues.

There was but one step to pass from these acts of administrative violence to plain and downright robbery. It became a crime to have been fortunate in the operations which Government itself had so much encouraged. A list was prepared of suspected persons, which is said to have comprised 35,000 names, and proceedings were commenced against them, some victims being selected to intimidate the rest and force them to give up their wealth. If we are curious to know how justice proceeded, the advocate Barbier explains it in a few words: "They enter a man's house: put a seal on everything: take from him his jewels, his plate, and everything he has." A vague terror paralysed business, and the most melancholy comedy was played before the eyes of the people. A number of persons, wealthy and of good repute, proclaimed themselves ruined, and studied to look the very pictures of misery. Chance discovered a stun of 500,000 livres in gold in a garret, where there was but a wretched pallet and two straw chairs.

Plays and Misery

As a contrast so striking that all the chroniclers have noticed it, never had the theatres been so much frequented and so brilliant as during these days of fearful distress. Marais writes, under date of 20th November:—"I have been to see the comedy which was played at the Palais Royal Theatre, where Baron represents the *Earl of Essex*. There were an immense number of people there in spite of the distress of the times. The women were covered with jewels, (the use of them had just been permitted again, and they smothered themselves with them, from head to foot); the men had magnificent and superb dresses. The Regent appeared with his mistress on one side: the Duke with his on the other. Any one who only saw the interior of the theatre would fancy the country very rich; but on leaving it the poverty is plain enough."

The receipts of the Opera rose from 60,000 to 740,188 livres in 1720. It is true that the taste for masked balls burst forth in this year. A Carmelite, whose religious name was Father Sebastian, may be considered the inventor of the Opera balls. It is he who first conceived the idea of raising the floor of the pit to a level with the stage so as to make the whole theatre into one great dancing saloon. This ingenious mechanism was inaugurated by the first ball on the 2nd of January, 1716. The rage for them showed itself three years later. "In the midst of this distress" says Marais, again in November, 1720, "they have opened the ball at the Opera which has been given publicly for three years, and where each person pays six livres. The ball lasted till seven in the morning. Many people were there on St. Martin's eve, and got rid of their Banknotes, losing nearly the whole value of them to go and dance, while they were starving at home. Such are Frenchmen and Parisians!"

And, nevertheless, the public distress appeared so irremediable, that it approached despair. Here is an example, cited by Buvat. On the 16th of December the Vicar of St. Eustache presiding over a charitable meeting, sent assistance to a family that had just been recommended to him. The person entrusted with this pious mission receiving no reply, forced open the door. "On entering the room he was surprised to see the husband hanged, and his wife and three children with their throats cut. In this room were found only six sous in coin, and banknotes for 200,000 livres, which were said to arise from the paying off the annuities in the Hotel de Ville. This unfortunate family were buried the following night at the cemetery of the Innocents, without any other search."

Departure of Law—His End

The situation of the man who was considered responsible for all these sufferings had become intolerable. His head, it was said everywhere, must be the price of the inevitable reconciliation of the Parliament and the Regency. One last proof put an end to Law's irresolutions. On the 12th of November, having appeared at the Bank, they threw in his teeth the names of robber and cheat. He retired with haughty bearing and a contemptuous glance, no longer thinking of anything but preparing for his retreat.

He possessed fourteen fine signorial estates, and large capital; but he was enormously in debt. He gave his power of attorney to the Grand Prior of Vendôme, begging him to make, in his name, an honourable liquidation. "He was so little attached to his property," says his anonymous apologist, "that he offered them to be distributed among those who might have suffered by his operations, and he wished to retain only an income of 30,000 francs. This offer was admired and rejected, because they had less desire to help the unfortunate than they had to destroy him."

In a secret conference that he had with the Regent, he gave him his last advice on the financial situation, and begged him to choose for Controller-General M. de la Houssaye, Chancellor of the house of Orleans. The latter, to obtain this office, had given Law to understand that he would be guided by his advice; but the very day after his installation, he proposed to the Prince, as a means of popularity, to throw the author of the *Scheme* into the Bastille: the Regent refused.

On the 12th of December, Law showed himself at the Opera. He was there an object of ill-willed curiosity, to which he opposed his English coolness. Having withdrawn next day to his estate of Guermande, he received a visit there from the Duke de Bourbon. On the 16th, Madame de Prie sent him her post-chaise with a passport in the King's name. Of the three millions which he had brought into France, and the enormous riches he had there acquired, Law then only possessed 36,000 livres, arising from an unexpected payment made to him, and two rings of the value of 10,000 crowns each, one of which he sent to Madame de Prie in gratitude for the service she had just rendered him. He set out at length for Brussels, where he was honourably received. His wife soon after joined him, after having realised sufficient to pay the small debts. The funded property was afterwards sold at a very low price, and nothing of it ever reached the fugitive.

On the 17th of December the Parliament was recalled to Paris.

Whilst Law was making for Brussels, concealed at the

bottom of a post-chaise, another post-chaise was following his. This one was occupied by a M. de Pressy, a Russian agent, who, having at length overtaken the author of the *Scheme*, placed in his hands despatches from the Czar, who begged him to come and take the direction of his finances.

Protected by the title of minister of France in Bavaria, and still more by the high idea which had been formed in Europe of his genius and honesty, Law lived honourably in foreign countries. From Brussels he went to Italy; made some trips to Germany, Denmark, and England, and at last settled in Venice, where he resided until his death, which happened in 1729. They fancied in France that he had carried away a treasure. Dubois, who had become his enemy, sent to Venice a certain Abbé de la Riviere, to watch the ex-Controller of Finance in the minutest details. The spy could discover nothing which was unfavourable to him. The truth is, that Law, returning to the trade to which he owed his first wealth, lived by play; this was no cause of reproach in Venice. He left at his death only a few pictures, and the 10,000 crowns' ring, which he used to pledge when the chances of the green table went against him.

Funeral Oration of the Scheme

The departure of Law having finally put an end to the *Scheme*, its history was summed up in the following genealogy, which was placarded on the walls of Paris:—

Beelzebub begat Law;
Law begat the Mississippi;
The Mississippi begat the Scheme;
The Scheme begat the paper;
The paper begat the Bank;
The Bank begat the note;
The note begat the share;

The share begat the stockjobbing;
The stockjobbing begat the registration;
The registration begat the account;
The account begat the general balance;
The balance begat zero;
From which all power of begetting was taken away.

CHAPTER VIII

AFTER THE SCHEME

CHAPTER VIII

AFTER THE SCHEME

Recriminations

About one month after Law's departure, a manuscript piece was passed about from hand-to-hand in public, which, doubtless, excited a lively curiosity, for several copies of it are still. found in the papers of the time.[1] It was a kind of minutes of transactions of a council of the Regency, held at the Tuilleries on the 26th of January, 1721, among twenty-eight persons, in the number of which figured the King, the Regent, the Princes of the blood, and the highest dignitaries. The object was to inquire into the position of the finances. The Duke of Bourbon having said that the notes in circulation were much more numerous than they had dared to confess to the public, the Regent replied, "that the excess of the notes had been caused by decrees of the council issued secretly: that Law had had 600 millions worth of them made without even secret decrees: that, to render them

---

1. It was afterwards discovered that the author of this scandal was the Duke de Saint-Simon, on finding it reproduced almost literally in his memoirs.

valid, it had been necessary to issue a decree which had to be ante-dated: that, for that and other things, Law deserved to have been hanged fifty times over."

This explanation, we must say, was more dishonouring to him who gave it than to the fugitive, for it bore the character of falsehood. The Duke of Bourbon dwelt long and with much power on the want of probability in the excuse alleged by the Regent to free himself from blame. "If Law had caused these notes to be made without your orders," said he, in conclusion, "you would not have procured him passports; you would not have hidden a capital crime in this manner." No reply was possible to this argument.

The new Controller of Finance, M. de la Houssaye put an end to this altercation by reading the report he had prepared. He presented things under the most sombre aspect. Eighty thousand most honourable families, he said, had been obliged to exchange their property for paper. To preserve them from despair, it was necessary to give their paper some value: the only means of doing that was to submit to a severe examination the shares and notes with which the place was inundated; and to destroy, without pity, all the securities whose origin was not free from the stain of stockjobbing. On these conclusions, the council decided that all the securities should undergo a *Visa*, in the form adopted in 1716, to reduce the papers created by Louis XIV.

The decree, instituting the *Visa*, appeared on the 4th of February, 1721. It obliged the holders of papers to submit them to control by declaring on what title they held these things, what value they had given for them, and whence came the sums laid out in the purchase of them. All the securities not presented before the month of August would be declared cancelled and of no value.

The announcement of such a measure spread general

consternation. As everyone had paper, everyone had a loss to submit to in perspective. The remembrance of the Chamber of Justice above all terrified the great shareholders. But as it is not in the nature of popular masses to be desperately interested in many things at a time, a new event made them forget the *Visa* for a time.

Forestallers

At the time when the shopkeepers could no longer keep up their supplies, and the scarcity of necessaries was causing anxiety even among rich families, it was learnt that considerable forestallments had just been discovered. The masters and keepers of the company of grocers being informed that individuals newly admitted into their corps were carrying on suspicious operations, had exercised a surveillance, and stated that their faithless brethren derived their goods from the Convent of the Grands Augustins. Having, therefore, requested the assistance of a commissary of the Châtelet and a file of archers, they presented themselves, on the 13th of February, at the gate of the convent, with the power of making a search there. Arrived at the grand hall, where sat, in 1716, that Chamber of Justice so dreaded by the embezzlers of public money, they found, in considerable quantities, goods belonging to their trade, such as sugar, coffee, spices, soaps, tallow, candles, wax, torches; other rooms, transformed into warehouses, contained tin, lead, copper, leather, and charcoal. Lastly, in the cellars were fifty large casks of brandy.

To whom did these stores belong? On asking the monks they were told that the purchases had been ordered by a M. Bénard, advocate in Parliament, and man of business to the Duke de la Force, and by the steward and many servants of the same Duke; that the purchases went back to a period anterior to the depreciation of the Banknotes, and that many millions had been employed in them.

Once on the trace of the monopolists they discovered on several sides stores of the same kind. The great Convent of the Cordeliers, as well as that of the Augustins, had been transformed into an *entrepôt*. We are assured that more than sixty stores of groceries were seized in private houses. Two boats laden with *eau-de-vie* were declared lawful prizes. Urged into rivalry by the example of the grocers, other corporations made discoveries: the chandlers learnt that a great store of tallow existed. The china-dealers laid hands on twenty-two cases of beautiful porcelain. On the 27th of March they seized, in a cellar of Mount St. Genevieve, more than 500,000 livres worth of Spanish wines and 200 tons of Virginian leaf tobacco. Searches made in many provincial towns, and especially in Orleans and Toulouse, led to similar discoveries.

Public indignation burst forth with such force from the very first day, that no one dared to claim property in the seized goods; the silence of the monopolists confirmed the severity of the judges. Suspicions hovered over several Mississippian nobles, especially the Duke d'Antin, the Duke de Guiche, and the Marshall d'Estrées. The only one proceeded against was the monopoliser of the Augustin Convent. It was a tremendous affair as yet, to call to account M. de la Force, Duke and Peer of France, president of finance and trade, and member of the Supreme Council of the Regency.

On the 15th of February the Parliament held an extraordinary meeting; and, on the petition of the grocers, declared the seizure of the goods good and valid, and awarded half of them to the Hospitals of Paris, and the other half to the informers, sentenced to a fine, and declared deprived of their freedom of the city, those grocers who had clandestinely purchased these goods to retail them. As for the Duke de la Force, being cited before the Parliament, and obliged to give up his sword before submitting to examination, he threw the whole blame on his steward, who, he said, had acted on his own authority. It was difficult to believe that a steward would have purchased groceries for several millions without his master's order. Nevertheless, they condemned the too zealous servant to the galleys. The penalty was afterwards commuted.

Although the disgrace of this judgment fell on the Duke de la Force, most of the dukes and peers did not consider him sufficiently punished; they intended to degrade their colleague from his rank, when a decree of removal to a superior tribunal took the matter out of the hands of Parliament, and commissioned four princes of the blood, four dukes and peers, and four councillors, to judge the noble culprit. The company of grocers having, by a formal order of the King, desisted from its suit, the Duke got off with a reprimand and the loss of his goods, which remained confiscated.

The *Visa*—Method and Results

As people were then in full reaction against the *Scheme*, they hastened to prevent the only good that could accrue from it. All administrative and fiscal reforms were suspended. Contractors were again allowed to collect the taxes. Nearly all the toll and import duties on provisions of the least necessity were re-established, as well as most of those offices, the temporary suppression of which had been so profitable to Parisian trade.

Without official titles, the brothers Paris had at this time the supreme direction of affairs. Their hateful influence was especially shown in the decision which was arrived at regarding the Indian Company. Though it never acted but under the orders of Government, since Law himself was an agent of power, the shareholders were declared responsible for all the engagements undertaken, and all the notes issued; sequestration was laid on all its property, and its affairs provisionally carried on by persons appointed by Government.

This act, severe even to injustice, was one of the preliminaries of the Visa. With the exception of a most trifling minority, there were no families who had not property arising from the Scheme, either because they had speculated in public securities, or because they had been subjected to a forced conversion of their annuities, offices, or credits. To classify these securities, to establish their filiation so as to fix their origin as more or less moral, was a gigantic work. The brothers Paris displayed great talent and firmness in it. They employed nine millions in the payment of an army of clerks army is the proper word, for it appears that they placed in the offices a number of bullies whose special duty it was to make ill-tempered suitors show proper respect. As it was necessary that the eye of some calculator of uncommon powers should glance over this ocean of papers and figures, they chose the celebrated Barême.

Seven sorts of securities were submitted to examination, comprising perpetual, life, and provincial annuities, banknotes, and various credits of the Bank and the Indian Company. Of all these they formed five categories determined by their origin, namely:—

1. Reimbursements made by the King;
2. Between private individuals;
3. Sales of immovable property;
4. Sales of furniture, goods, appointments, wages, salaries, and manual gifts; and
6. Origins undeclared.

Numerous sub-divisions were further made under each of these categories.

It was decided that the securities thus classed, should lose more or less according as their origin was more or less suspicious. The annuities arising from reimbursements made by the King were not reduced. The other securities had to undergo a progressive loss from one-sixteenth to nineteen-twentieths.

Not only were the declarations to be made on oath, but notaries were ordered, under pain of being deprived of their offices and prosecuted extraordinarily, to furnish extracts from all deeds transferring property, such as lands, furniture, annuities, appointments, and offices from the 1st of July, 1719, to the 31st of December, 1720. Only deeds of private life such as marriage contracts, wills, and inventories after death, were exempted from control. Such an inquisition was unprecedented. It was considered necessary to discover the changes of fortunes, and the honesty of the transactions.

The papers arrived by bushels from all parts of the country. The bundles deposited, to the number of 511,009, represented a capital of 3,122,236,436 livres. In this sum the shares of the Company, to the number of 125,024, were valued by the holders at 900 millions. The contracts of annuities and accounts in the Bank figured for nearly a billion; the Banknotes for 1,200 to 1,300 millions.

The first sitting of the Commissary Judges took place on the 16th of December, 1721, and the work was pushed on with such vigour that, by the month of March following, it had decided on 300,000 affairs. The operations were terminated in 1722, but were not finally closed until September, 1728.

The holders of paper had been divided into two classes; first, those who possessed more than 10,000 livres; and secondly, those who possessed less than that sum. The second group comprised 460,000 heads of families, nearly all small tradesmen, artisans, and servants. For these people the losses were made as small as possible. In the number of people reputed rich were reckoned about 51,000 individuals. The annuitants, whose annuities had been converted in spite of themselves, and still overwhelmed with their paper capital, suffered no reduction; they were only obliged to reinvest their capital in annuities at a disadvantageous rate. Lastly, there remained to the number of about 40,000 the fortunate speculators, tauntingly called "new men." The securities presented by these were classed in the category of suspicious ones, and in great part cancelled.

To sum up, according to Paris Duverney, the principal director of the operation, the cancellings amounted to 522 millions in notes and contracts, and 498 millions in shares. The securities preserved represented still 1,700 millions, which, transformed into perpetual annuities at 2 and one-half percent, or life annuities at 4 percent, produced thirty-one millions of the first, and sixteen millions of the second. These figures show the total amount of the public debt after the grand liquidation which followed the *Scheme*.

As for the Indian Company, the number of shares judged worthy of being preserved amounting to 56,000, the Society was reconstructed within these limits. It became a private enterprise devoted to the working of many commercial monopolies; and it was calculated that, under these conditions, it might supply a dividend of 150 livres on each of its retained shares.

Poll-Tax Extraordinary

A sacrifice of a billion had first been forced on the new men. It was considered that they were still not hit hard enough by the reductions made of their depreciated paper. It was determined to touch them in a more direct way. A decree of the Council ordered that there should be levied a *poll-tax extraordinary* on those who had realised considerable profits. A Royal Chamber was installed at the arsenal, with the commission to tax arbitrarily speculators pointed out as millionaires, either by their notorious wealth, or by secret informations. Four hundred names soon figured on the provisional list.

These preliminaries spread terror among the *par-venues*. Each one tried to get exempted through the protection of great people, which gave rise to scenes both sad and comic, but always scandalous. Bachelors went in search of what were called *young ladies of protection*, that is, girls of birth, but poor, and bringing no dowry but family influence. Others, no longer marriageable, bargained for the influence of some female intriguer. The most fortunate were those who, finding that some powerful man wished for their house, or one of their estates, or an appointment to be purchased at great cost, found means to make their homage acceptable by supplying them.

These manoeuvres succeeded with many people. Fifty-nine of the largest millionaires escaped the tax; and, among the number, the names of fourteen are mentioned who were said to have a joint fortune of 330 millions. The others, in general less rich, paid for all. The capitation lists of the 15th of September, 1722, comprising the taxes arranged in order for some tens of thousands of livres to eight millions, (it was Madame Chaumont who reached this figure,) produced a total of 187,893,000 livres. The persons thus mulcted had first lost in the *Visa* the greater part of their securities in hand. They were not the less rigorously prosecuted for payment of their full tax, so that many were obliged, in order to liberate themselves, to sell their lands at a low price. This was not all. The aristocracy bitterly regretted the fine hotels and estates of which they had been dispossessed. To console them, permission was given to the former sellers to buy back their patrimonial property by paying for it in contracts for annuities at par, or in securities consolidated by the *Visa*. All these measures overwhelmed those who were not supported by favour. Many Mississippians, then habituated to extravagant luxury, fell back again to that obscurity from which they had raised themselves by their industry.

As soon as the verifications of the *Visa* were finished, they had a large iron cage erected in the court-yard of the Bank, in which a fire was lighted, and for several days, registers, accounts, in fact all the materials of its labours, were thrown into it. In this way, under pretence of smothering family secrets in the flames, they cut short all after appeals.

Betrayals of Trust

Scarcely were the first certificates of liquidation delivered, when they were negotiated at sixty percent premium. But suddenly the place was so inundated with them, that they fell below par. Some fraud was suspected, and it was discovered that two commissary judges, M. Talhouet, Master of Requests, and the Abbé Clement, Councillor in the Grand Council, had an understanding with the clerks to reject the demands of certain suitors, and that they sold the certificates for their own benefit. It was necessary to create at the Arsenal a kind of Star Chamber to judge the dishonest judges of the Royal Chamber. Talhouet and Clement being people of rank were condemned to be beheaded, and their two principal accomplices to be hanged like small folks as they were. Fortunately for these four thieves, the brother of the Abbé Clement was accoucheur of the Queen of Spain. The King, Philip V, solicited so earnestly the Abbé's pardon that they were obliged, to save this one's head, to commute the punishment of the other three. The two judges got off with imprisonment, and the clerks with banishment. As for the robbed families, they could never get any compensation. The loss they sustained was computed at thirty millions.

Such deeds, which would raise public indignation nowadays, seemed much less revolting in 1722, so general and deep-rooted was the demoralisation. The overthrow of all existing things, unbridled extravagance in the midst of frightful distress, the habit of gain without labour, the passion for play, the shameless debauchery, the abuses of power; and, above all, the bad example of the highest had disturbed all conscience, and confounded all notions of good and evil. So many people had been robbed most pitilessly, that a great number of all classes had come to consider Society as a cutthroat, and considered they were only taking in reprisals in helping themselves to other people's property. At no period have robberies and murders been so frequent as during the period which elapsed between the departure of Law and the death of the Regent. And as people are accustomed in their own way to make a synthesis of events which strike them, and to concentrate on one head the sentiments which excite them, they attributed all the crimes to the influence of a cutthroat, who has become a kind of myth under the name of Cartouche.

Anecdotes like the following, feeding curiosity, spread the contagion of terror from the last months of 1721.

The Accomplices of Cartouche

It was the commencement of winter. An old gentleman, passing along the Rue des Mathurins St. Jacques, was stopped by two robbers, who in an instant took away his hat, wig, watch, sword, and purse filled with twelve louis d'or. It was nine in the evening, the district was dark and deserted, and when any one knocked at a door to ask for help, the inhabitants might be heard locking themselves in. The robbed gentleman seeking vainly from house to house for an asylum, arrived half dead with fear and cold at the Hotel de Cluny, then inhabited by M. de Verthamont, president of the Grand Council. This Magistrate having recognised in the suppliant a man of rank, received him graciously, repaired the disorder of his dress, and made him accept an invitation to supper, promising to send him back to his house in his carriage. The supper hour arrived. The nobleman being presented to the company by his host took his place at the table, and to satisfy the curiosity of the guests, began again the recital of his mishap. By degrees his face grew pale, his voice trembled and was hushed; no sound was heard but of his teeth chattering. He at last gave them to understand that feeling unwell he wished to retire. The President offered him his arm to lead him to a bedchamber. As soon as they were alone the nobleman declared that his two robbers were among the number of the guests: that he recognised them perfectly, though they had changed their clothes. Fancying himself the dupe of an intriguer or the victim of a madman, the President assumed a severe air, and said, "Your words are very grave, sir: have you sufficiently reflected on them? The two persons whom you accuse, I would have you to know are connections of mine." The nobleman persisting in his declaration, M. de Verthamont "sent for a locksmith, and while the company were finishing supper, had the rooms of the individuals in question opened, and there found the stolen things. On which, a commissary having arrived with some archers, the two robbers were arrested at table, and conveyed to the Châtelet, to the great astonishment of the company."[2]

During two years nothing was talked of in France but Cartouche and his accomplices. This incarnate demon passed for having allies in all parts of the kingdom, in all classes of society, and the fearful affair of the Count de Horn, remembered by all, excused the credulity of the timid. Whether many robbers really belonged to the distinguished classes, or they took disguises adapted to the parts they had to play, there were pointed out, in the number of arrests mentioned from day to day by the chroniclers, people of rank, priests of rank, bodyguards, persons attached to the establishments of the King and the Princes, two sergeants and four soldiers of the French guards, the guard at the Bank, many citizens and especially goldsmiths, the son of a well-known bookseller, and many notaries' clerks. A pretty flowerseller, much sought after by the frequenters of

---

2. Buvat.

the Opera, was hanged, and a few days later a woman living near the church of St. Paul, and looked upon as almost a saint in the parish. This one, listening at night to the signals of the robbers, used to drop a rope from her window, which she drew up when they had fastened to it a basket containing objects of value. "It is declared," says Buvat, "that a woman, when in the Conciergerie, has declared to the judges that if they will promise her her life, with perpetual imprisonment, she will denounce more than six hundred persons of distinction who have carriages, or are considered wealthy citizens." Cartouche himself was seized on the information of one of his principal accomplices, Louis Duchatelet, who, adds Barbier quite seriously, was a "very good gentleman."

The Provinces were no safer than Paris. Carriages were stopped on the roads. The forests were full of brigands, of whom frightful stories are related. The Cartouche of the South was a certain Pellissier, of Lyons, who called himself a Marquis, and led a splendid life. His connections with high society and men of business, gave him opportunities of giving information to the brigands, who acted under his orders. This dreaded man was brought to Paris from Lyons in one of his own carriages, drawn by six of his horses. The procession was completed by two other carriages and two carts, in which they had stowed his accomplices, men and women. They were all hanged on the Place de Grève on the 10th and 11th of July, 1722. Among the number was noticed a woman of rare beauty, who was said to be the daughter of a banker in Lyons. This was not the only time they brought malefactors to Paris by cartloads.

The public loudly crying out for the speedy destruction of the whole brood of Cartouche, the judges acted with a haste and an excess of severity which perhaps occasioned cruel reprisals. Nothing was heard of but arrests, tortures, and executions during the year 1722. The condemned, all offering to make confessions to prolong their agony, comprised a number of persons. Simple robbers were hanged: murderers broken on the wheel. The precautions taken to prevent some criminals from being recognised, made people suppose that they feared to disgrace honourable names. Barbier writes, in his journal: "It is the fashion now to hang robbers by torch-light; two have just passed by my door at ten at night: there were two dozen of torches to each."

Stockjobbing is Revived—The Hotel des Quatre Provinces

In 1721, in the uncertainty as to the result of the mysterious operations of the *Visa*, from six to ten livres were given for a note of one hundred livres, and forty to one hundred livres for a share. These exchanges gave rise to a traffic from which the skilful derived great profits.

As soon as the results of the *Visa* were known, the capitalists, brokers, and jobbers again began to speculate in these new securities. The meetings were then held in the Quartier Saint Martin, where the streets and refreshment houses were literally besieged. No longer willing or able to stop these dealings, Government sought to regulate them by assigning to them an official place in the Rue St. Martin, and known as the Hotel des Quatre Provinces. Immediately all the lodgings in the place were turned into offices. The shares of the new Indian Company, levied by decree at 56,000, were represented by provisional certificates of the value of 500 livres; these certificates were soon negotiated at 800 livres, which were paid for in gold with astonishing facility. Louis, of different coinages, and of very different values, reappeared as if they sprang from the earth. Each speculator, furnished with scales, weighed and valued the pieces offered to him immediately. Time bargains became the rage. People bought at a premium from day to day, advancing as much as one hundred francs on a share of 500 livres. This soon made the shares rise to 1,200 livres; they reached 1,500 when it was learned that the Company had recovered the tobacco monopoly. The jobbers declared every morning that the Regent regretted the *Scheme*, and longed to re-establish it. Rogues promised dupes the return of Law, who, they said, had invented in exile a *paper of confidence*, destined to revive the prosperous days of the Rue Quincampoix.

Thus, was the terrible punishment of the follies of the *Scheme* already forgotten! Let no one be surprised at it! Nothing demoralises a people so speedily as the facility of gain without labour. The excitement of gambling had become so necessary to many people, that *roulette* was invented for the use of those who were not satisfied with the daily profits of the Hotel des Quatre Provinces. Roulette, established 1723 in the Hotels de Gresvres and de Soissons, lasted till 1830. Who could count its victories during its 107 years of existence?

Dispersion of the Mississippians

The sudden death of the Regent, (on the 3rd of December, 1723) threw the stockjobbers into consternation by dissipating their illusions. The shares fell instantly to 900 livres. Nevertheless, people in a position to see the cards were noticed to play for the rise more than ever. In the month of March, 1724, the secret of this manoeuvre appeared. A decree of the Council conferred on the Indian Company the privilege of placing the annuity shares into a lottery; this combination, attributed to Law, was very seductive to the public, promising large profits to the speculators. At first there was such a burst of enthusiasm that the shares sprang up to above 3,000 livres. But, suddenly, decrees appearing to modify the legal value of the coinage, spread confusion in the camp of professional stockjobbers. A frightful fall took place, and threw into despair those who had bought at high prices.

Contemporaries believed that these moves, concealed in profound secrecy, had been managed for the profit of a few great nobles, who, perceiving in the new administration tendencies very little in favour of stockjobbing, had begged them to bring about one more rise, so that they might realise on good terms. In support of this suspicion, they allege that a servant of the house of de Rohain had gained 900,000 livres by playing for the rise, in a manner that would have been mad if he had not been in his masters' secrets.

The shares had fallen from 3,000 livres to 1,500 in a day, when there appeared, at twenty days interval, (the 24th of September and the 14th of October) two decrees of the Council establishing a regular Commercial Exchange, out of which no transactions could take place, and conferring on sixty exchange agents the monopoly of purchases and sales. Judging in an absolute manner, this was a progress. But to close without previous notice the ordinary place of these transactions, to fetter the freedom of contracts, to break through habits already inveterate, this was only removing the basis of operations, and preventing people of good faith from the possibility of honouring their engagements. Government remained deaf to representations of this kind. They gave chase more keenly than ever to those who chose to dispense with the intervention of an exchange agent. Some rash people, meeting in retired places, like disciples of a forbidden religion, jobbed among themselves, waiting for martyrdom in the shape of the rude correction of the police. In short, the shares fell to below 500 francs, never to rise again, and the lottery never took place which had so inflamed people's imaginations.

Thus ended the financial period over which domineered the genius of Law.

CHAPTER VIII

What Should we Think of Law?

Was the career of the Scotch adventurer useful or hurtful to France? This problem could not be solved by a plain and absolute reply. A movement so complicated, a change so thorough, and phenomena so strange, authorises the most contradictory opinions. Impressions change with the point of view. To form a strictly impartial and thoroughly reasonable judgment, the premises to be considered would form a volume as large as the recital of these facts.

The heart is torn at beholding the dreadful effects of an earthquake. A few years afterwards we see on the same spot a city more beautiful, more smiling, more rich than that which has been destroyed. We forget the victims who have disappeared while admiring the prosperity of the generation before our eyes. Such are the impressions we undergo when examining, not the rapid episode of Law, but the eighteenth century in its *ensemble*.

As a financier, Law has almost always been judged by the writings of his mortal enemy, Paris Duverney. It is on this authority we are so often told that the treasury was left in debt, after Law's departure, 658 millions more than at the death of Louis XIV. But Paris Duverney, good calculator as he was, allowed himself to be blinded by passion. In the account of the deficit, created by Louis XIV, he has not reckoned the enormous floating debt which the *Scheme* absorbed. As for the consolidated debt, it is clear that the interest of it was lessened, since it passed from 4 percent to 2 and one-half percent; and since certain offices, for which the treasury had to provide annuities, were suppressed.

But, it will be thought, if the State as debtor, gained—the subjects as creditors, must have lost? The conclusion would be just in our times, when the State religiously pays its debts. It was not so under the *ancien régime*. Before the *Scheme* the annuities were constituted at 4 to 5 percent; but they were so badly paid, that half was lost in realising the capital. After the *Scheme*, the lowered interest was discharged much more regularly. In law, the forced conversion of 1719 was a bankruptcy; in fact, the annuitants suffered more fear than real evil. The real bankruptcy arose from the debasing of the coinage, which, from 1715 to 1726, lessened the coined livre 80 per cent; but in this operation, which the ignorance of the times excused, Law was not the only one guilty.

If some individuals were damaged in the overthrow, it is incontestable that the thorough change of capital fertilised the national soil. Nearly all debtors, and especially landlords weighed down with mortgages, discharged their debts. Many ancient domains were raised from ruin, and many new buildings erected. The soil received lasting improvements. Industry, keenly excited, raised new manufactures. The example of maritime speculations was given by the Indian Company. Lastly, in spite of that exportation of precious metals which frightened it, France soon found itself richer in gold and silver than any country in Europe. The Regent left ninety-one millions in specie in the treasury at his death: and it is declared that at the grand recoinage of money in 1726, Paris alone brought more money to the mint than all Great Britain possessed.

How could these favourable results spring from a sad catastrophe? An impartial judge, and one very enlightened, M. Gautier, deputy-governor of the Bank, shall make us understand it:—"Law's conception, in spite of its original vices, which rendered its success impossible, in spite of the blind temerity and grave faults which rendered its fall so sudden and so terrible, still bears evidence of its author possessing, besides a powerful and inventive genius, the distinct perception of the three most fertile, and till then most ignored, sources of the greatness of nations—maritime commerce, credit, and the spirit of association."

In the obscurity of his exile, Law again wrote to the Regent:—"Do not forget that the introduction of credit has brought more change among the powers of Europe than the discovery of the Indies: that it is for the sovereign to give and not to receive it, and that the people have so absolute a need of it, that they return to it in spite of themselves, and whatever distrust they may have of it." In these few words, a mixture of errors and truths, experienced eyes will read the secret of Law's strength and his weakness, his success and his fall. No, it is not the office of the State to distribute credit itself: but its duty should be to procure it for all, in lessening the obstacles and destroying the monopolies which stand in the way of its wide distribution. Credit is so fruitful in its nature, that, even when it is pushed to inordinate exaggerations, as in Law's experiment, it leaves a lasting progress after passing sufferings.

The *Scheme*, by inflaming avarice, contributed to the demoralisation of the country. Still, it would be unjust to accuse Law personally, who showed himself more honest, and especially more disinterested than most of those with whom he came in contact. Besides, must not the germs of corruption have existed everywhere, for its growth to have been so rapid and so general? We have attempted here to lift only a corner of the veil, just as much as was necessary to throw light on the financial movement of the first years of the eighteenth century, and the little we have shown will give a sad idea of the times. Sordid avarice, abuse of power, extortion, violence, the monstrous perversity of some natures—these composed an *ensemble* such as (to the honour of our own times, be it said) will make many readers of these pages regard their recital as improbable. To what are we to attribute that incontestable progress of public morality, if not to a more generally extended education, and a sentiment of dignity based on institutions more judicious and more equitable? Let us, then, apply ourselves to ameliorate the present, which, doubtless, leaves much for us to do, while freeing ourselves from the regrets which ignorance alone feels for past times.

INDEX

Academy of Sciences 86
Aix 22, 71
Amsterdam 27, 28, 38
Anti-Scheme 45, 46, 53, 60, 61, 69, 137
Argyll, Duke of 25, 28

Bandoliers 106
banknotes, *see* Mississippi Scheme: bank, national (Royal): banknotes, and, Mississippi Scheme: bank, private (General): banknotes
Bank of England 26
Barbier's Journal 133
Bastille 7, 13, 56, 158
Bayle's Dictionary 100
Bernardines 4
Bernard, Samuel 4, 15
Bignon, Abbé 117
Bordeaux 22, 71, 77, 110
Bourbon, Duke de, 47, 78, 112, 127, 132, 150, 158, 163, 164
Bourvalais 12, 13, 14, 20
Broglie, Duc de, 137
Brussels 29, 71, 121, 158, 159

Campbell, Jane, *see* Law, Jane, *mother*
Carignau, Prince de, 152
Cartouche 151, 173, 174, 175
Chamber of Justice 7, 8, 10, 13, 14, 15, 16, 18, 19, 20, 21, 22, 35, 39, 45, 91, 165
Chaumont, Madame 75, 84, 171
Clement, Abbé 172

Colbert 3, 7, 54, 55
Company, Indian, *see* Mississippi Scheme: Company, Indian
Company, Mississippi, *see* Mississippi Scheme: Company, Indian
Company, Western, *see* Mississippi Scheme: Company, Western
Considerations on Currency and Commerce 28
Conti, Prince de, 78, 79, 112
Council of Administration 61
Crozat, Antoine 15, 41, 54, 57, 85

d'Aguesseau, *Chancellor of France* 8, 40, 78, 137, 148
Dalesne, Monsieur 77
d'Antin, Duke 47, 78, 166
d'Aremberg, Duke 115, 116
d'Argenson, Monseiur 11, 29, 40, 43, 44, 45, 46, 60, 132, 137
debased 153
de la Force, Duke, 165, 166, 167
de la Houssaye, Monsieur 158, 164
de la Mark, Count 89
de la Riviere, Abbé 159
de Pressy, Monsieur 159
Desmarets, *Controller General of France* 4, 11, 30
d'Estreés, Marshall 78, 166
d'Evreux, Count 15, 85
Duclos, *actress* 29
Dumoulin, *War Treasurer* 16–17
Duval, Abbé 76
Duverney, Paris 170, 179

education, grants for 92
Exchange Alley 87, 88

Farmers of the Revenue 8, 16, 45, 46, 62
Florence 27, 30
Fourqueux, de, *Attorney-General* 8

Genoa 27, 30
Gruet, Monseiur 10–12
Guermande 100, 158
Guiche, Duke de, 166

Horn, Count de, 119–122, 130, 174
Hotel de Gesvres 29
Hotel de Mesme 37

Hotel de Nevers 14
Hotel de Ville 22, 134, 157
Hotel Mazarin 14

Indian Company, *see* Mississippi Scheme: Company, Indian

Lafare, Marquis of, 12
La Fontaine 150
Laforce, Duke de, 78
Lambert, Aimon 46, 60
La Rochefoucauld, Duke 15, 78
Lassé, Marquis de, 78
Lauriston, estate of 26
Law, Jane, mother 25
Law, John
  abilities 26, 27, 28
  Academy of Sciences, elected to 86
  adoration of 85–87
  appearance 26
  birth 25
  Catholicism, conversion to 99
  characteristics 26, 27, 28, 31, 88–89
  Considerations on Currency and Commerce 28
  contempt for 133, 137, 149, 157
  death of 159
  duel 27
  escape from prison 27
  estates, owneship of 100, 157
  flight from England 27
  France, escape from
    Brussels, arrival in 158
  gambling, and 25, 26, 27, 28, 29, 54
  legacy of 179–182
  Orleans, Duke of, and
    influence over 39
    introduced to 29
  sentenced to death 27
  social status 26
  speculation, responsibility for 73
  taxation, and 89–91
  territorial bank
    Council of Ministers
      proposal to 35–36

        rejection by 36
    Scotland
        proposed to 28–29
        rejection of 29
    titles, purchase of 100
    women, pestered by 86–87
Law, William, *father* 26
Louisiana, territory of 41–42, 55–57
Louis XIV 3, 4, 5, 6, 14, 15, 21, 22, 27, 30, 35, 41, 68, 85, 89, 164, 179
    France, financial condition of at death 35
    France, financial condition of during reign 4–6
Louis XV 22, 44, 148, 149
Louvois, Abbé de, 14

Mazarin Palace 61, 139, 140
Mississippi Company, *see* Mississippi Scheme: Company, Indian
Mississippi Scheme
    aftermath of 163–178
    bank, national (Royal)
        banknotes
            demand for 58
            depreciation of 100
            devaluation of 131
            forced use of 73, 111, 131
            forgery of 123
            loss of confidence in 110
            proliferation of 73, 130, 131
            value, decline of 135–136, 153
            withdrawal of 133, 134, 151–153
        branches of 52–53
        established 51
        reunited with India Company 127–128
    bank, private (General)
        banknotes
            benefits of 38–39
            introduction of 38
            Regent, support of 37, 39
            terms of 38
        charter, terms of 36–37
        established 36
        nationalized 51
        success of 38

Company, Indian
    conscription of poor and criminal 101–109
    established 54
    income, table of 63
    Louisiana territory, misrepresentation of 55–57
    number and value of shares issued, table of 63
    public revenue
        administration and collection of, rights granted 59–61
        administration and collection of, rights revoked 155
    reunited with royal bank 127–128
    revenue collection
        rights of 59–61
    shares
        cancellations 129, 134
        devaluation of 131, 132
        issues 57–63, 67
        price, apex of 75, 98
        price, fixed 129
        speculation in 58–60, 64, 71–72, 74, 77, 98, 130, 135, 152–153, 176–177
    tax exemptions, grant of 55
    trading privileges, acquision of 55, 58–59, 61
Company, Western
    Company, China, acquisition of 54
    Company, East Indian, acquisition of 54
    Company, Guinea, acquisition of 54
    established 42
    Louisiana, territory of, and 42, 55–57
    renamed Indian Company 54
    share buyback 53–54
    trading privileges, acquisition of 42, 54
duties, abolition of certain 90–91
edict of 21st of May 1720 131
    consequences of 132
    revocation of 132
effects of 100–101, 115–118, 146–149
end of 159–160
imitated in Europe 87
jewels, wearing prohibited 81, 98, 136
national debt
    conversion of 41, 43, 60–61
precious metals, restrictions of 98, 111, 133
public benefits of 91–93

    rioting 137–143
    shares, market for closed 130
    South Sea Scheme, inspired by 87–88
    specie
        abolition of 111–115, 130
        concealment of 111–115, 128, 133, 155–156
        devaluation of 43–44, 99, 110–111, 180
        rejection of 74
        restrictions in use of 111
    speculation, effects of 76, 79–85, 97
Molière 7

Naples 27
National Library of France 14, 61
Nigon, Monsieur 115, 116, 121
Noailles, Duke of, 7, 40
Nocé, Count de, 82
Normand, Monsieur le, 10–12

opera balls 156–157
Orleans, Duke of, 25, 29, 30, 79, 112, 117, 127, 146, 147, 149
  death of 177
  Law, John
    influenced by 39
    introduced to 29
    view of 39, 127, 137
  Regent of France 30
  threats against 149–150

Palace of Justice 21, 142, 144
Palatine, Princess, *mother of the Duke of Orleans* 79
paper money, *see* Mississippi Scheme: bank, national (Royal): banknotes,
    and, Mississippi Scheme: bank, private (General): banknotes
Paris, Brothers 45, 46, 53, 60, 113, 137, 167, 168
Parliament
  banishment of 143–146
  recall to to Paris 158
Philip V, King of Spain 172
Place de Grêve 175
Place des Victoires 130
Place Vendôme 13, 135, 136, 152
poll tax 170–172
Pontchartrain, *Chancellor of France* 16, 89, 112

Pontoise 144, 145, 146
Prie, Madame de, 158
Randleston, estate of 26
Rennes 22
Rome 27, 30, 68
Rouen 22, 110, 123
Rue de Richelieu 14, 61
Rue Quincampoix 68, 68–71, 69, 70, 71, 74, 75, 76, 78, 80, 86, 87, 98, 99, 119, 130, 135, 155, 177
Rue St. Honoré 81, 107, 142
Rue Vivienne 61, 67, 137, 139, 140, 141

Saint-Simon, Duc de, 19, 25, 27, 36, 78, 79, 103, 107, 146, 163
Smallpox 124
South Sea Company 88
Squadron, The 28

Turin 30

University of Paris 92

Vendôme, Duke de, 45
Venice 27, 30, 159
Vergier 150–151
Vermalet, Monsieur 18
Vernezobre, Monsieur 154–155
Vérue, Madame de, 78
Villeroy, Marshall de, 78
Visa 6, 22, 45, 69, 164, 164–170, 171, 176

Western Company, *see* Mississippi Scheme: Company, Western
Wilson, Edward 27

MORE FROM NEWTON PAGE

The Life of John Law
John Philip Wood
ISBN-13: 9781934619018

John Law of Lauriston: Financier and Statesman, Founder of the Bank of France, Originator of the Mississippi Scheme
A. W. Wiston-Glynn
ISBN-13: 9781934619032

**The Mississippi Bubble:
A Memoir of John Law**
Adolphe Thiers
ISBN-13: 9781934619056

**John Law's Money and Trade Considered:
A Hidden Foundation of Modern Economic Thought**
Gavin John Adams
ISBN-13: 9781934619094

Letters to John Law
Gavin John Adams
ISBN-13: 9781934619087

Newton Page books are available at all good bookstores and online book retailers. For more information about our books and how to order them, please visit our website:

www.newtonpage.com